Lead, Kindly
Light

A Mother's Escape from Communist
Russia During World War II
The Inspiring True Story
of Agnes Loewen

Lead, Kindly
Light

Helen Grace Lescheid

Pleasant Word
PW A Division of WinePress Group

First printing, June 1999
Second printing, May 2000
German edition, 2002, Brunnen Verlag, Giessen
Tenth Anniversary printing

Pleasant Word (a division of WinePress Publishing, PO Box 428, Enumclaw, WA 98022) functions only as book publisher. As such, the ultimate design, content, editorial accuracy, and views expressed or implied in this work are those of the author.

Unless otherwise noted, all Scriptures are taken from the *Holy Bible, New International Version*®, NIV®. Copyright © 1973, 1978, 1984 by the International Bible Society. Used by permission of Zondervan. All rights reserved.

ISBN 13: 978-1-4141-1356-2
ISBN 10: 1-4141-1356-0
Library of Congress Catalog Card Number: 2008910122

What People Are Saying About
Lead, Kindly Light

An absolutely riveting story...it was hard to put it aside.

What a tale of tragedy, grief, and redemption!

A deeply moving story of a woman's eternal power of survival.

A wonderfully compelling story of faith, perseverance, and God's provision.

A powerful witness of God's faithfulness and the human spirit's capacity to receive and respond to that infinite Goodness.

I'm having a hard time leaving the book and getting some needed housework done.

This book has encouraged me as a mother to never give up.

I couldn't put it down until I had read the whole book. It clearly shows how Neta acknowledged God's very personal leading, protection, and provision in her life.

It amazes me that one person could experience so much pain and struggle and come through it a loving, grateful, and humble person.

After reading the book, I realize how easy my life has been.

It will be my Christmas gift to a couple of teenage girls.

The book is a powerful reminder that, no matter how bad a situation, God is there.

Reading and rereading Neta's story has given me pause to examine my own journey to a deeper commitment to Christ.

An amazing story of determination, courage and faith.

Contents

Acknowledgments

M Y HEARTFELT THANKS goes to:

—Agnes Loewen, my mother, who recorded her memoirs in a scribbler for her grandchildren. They became the basis for this book.

—My siblings Agnes, Fred, and Katie and my aunt Anne (Dyck) Kessenich and great-aunt Anna Penner who shared their stories with me.

—Anne-Marie Nakhla, my niece, whose insightful editing and help with photography has been invaluable.

—Most of all, I thank my Father in heaven for His faithful presence and loving intervention in our lives for without Him there would be no story to tell.

Lead, Kindly Light, amid the encircling gloom,

Lead thou me on,

The night is dark, and I am far from home,

Lead thou me on.

Keep thou my feet: I do not ask to see

The distant scene: one step enough for me.

So long thy power hath blest me, sure it still

Will lead me on,

O'er moor and fen, o'er crag and torrent, till

The night is gone.

And with the morn those angel faces smile

Which I have loved long since, and lost awhile.

—John Henry Newman

Foreword

AT 87 YEARS old, my mother, Agnes Loewen (affectionately called Neta), radiated vitality and love of life. Despite great difficulties, she vehemently refused to feel sorry for herself.

During a return trip from a cancer clinic, I glimpsed a reason for her indomitable spirit. Because she was hard of hearing, I explained to her what the oncologist had said to her back in his office–the surgery had gone well. She had made a good recovery. There was no need for her to return for further checkups unless her family doctor found something suspicious in her chest again.

With a mischievous sparkle in her bright blue eyes, my mother said, "I don't think it was cancer in the first place."

"Mom, they wouldn't do surgery and go to all that expense if it weren't."

"Well, then, it's done me no harm," she said with finality.

Debilitating surgery forgotten, she'd accepted this trial as everything else in her tumultuous life, without self-pity or bitterness. And without those strong emotional ties holding her back, she'd already dismissed it as of no importance.

My mother's bout with cancer served as an added stimulus to get her life story into print. Painstakingly I translated her handwritten memoirs from German into English which became the basis for this book.

Although my mother had handwritten her memoirs as a legacy to her grandchildren, I felt *Lead, Kindly Light* deserved a wider audience. When my life veered out of control, I found courage in seeing how my mother had overcome insurmountable odds. Her quiet faith and perseverance helped me not to give up. Wouldn't other single parents find in its pages hope for their own lives?

I believed they would. Many enthusiastic readers have written me from different parts of the world of the blessings they have received. My prayer is that you, too, will find in the pages of this book hope and courage to keep looking to our Father of lights who is with us in every circumstance and shows us a way to survive and triumph.

Lead, Kindly Light was first published in Canada in 1999 and in Germany in 2002 under the title *Am Morgen lächeln die Engel*. My mother was able to read both versions before her death in May, 2003. In this tenth anniversary edition, I've expanded the text and included more photos.

Unfortunately, my mother showed great discomfort with the book and when people praised her for her courage. I put it down to her shyness: she hated it when people fussed over her. Later, I discovered a deeper reason. "You've told only the good parts about me," she said. "But I wasn't always good and brave. I have done many things wrong." Yes, of course. Neta did have her faults and her own childhood insecurities and needs. But I have chosen to focus on the many fine qualities of my mother. I feel she did the best she could under very adverse circumstances.

—Helen Grace Lescheid (Lena)
Abbotsford, British Columbia, Canada

Preface

SOME TIME AGO my daughter, Lena, with her young son, Jonathan, visited me. After a meal, I began to reminisce about the old days in my native Ukraine. My aunt Anna soon chimed in with her own remembrances.

"When I'm old, I'll write down my experiences," I said.

Jonathan, my grandson, grinned at me, "Oma, you'd better start right away," he said. "If you wait much longer, you'll have forgotten everything."

He may be right. I'm past eighty five now, and it's time to begin. I'm writing for my children and grandchildren. My earliest recollections may not be altogether factual, but I shall write it the way I remember it. Our lives were very different then—no cars, no radios, no television, no electricity...

The story begins...

PART ONE

An Alien in My Home Country (1912-1943)

Remember your journey...that you may know the righteous acts of the LORD
                                        —Micah 6:5b

CHAPTER ONE

My Childhood
in Chortitza

AS GERHARD DYCK held his infant child wrapped in a knitted blanket, he studied her little face as she slept: her rosy cheeks framed by a white knitted bonnet, wispy blond hair peeking out from under it, a tiny fist curled around an edge of her blanket. His heart swelled with pride at the sight of his firstborn child. The baby opened her eyes and focussed them on his gentle face as though she were eager to make the acquaintance of her father. *She has my blue eyes*, he smiled. *And my inquisitive nature.*

From the very beginning, a bond of love grew between my father and me. As he cradled me in his strong arms, I imagine him thinking *she's so frail, so vulnerable. Will I be able to provide for her adequately?* As a factory worker building plows, scythes, and other farm implements he was making a pretty good wage. But how long would it last? Russia was in political turmoil. Strikes and uprisings everywhere. He remembered "Bloody Sunday" when government troops had fired on a crowd of protesters and killed or wounded hundreds of marchers. But that had happened in Russia thousands of miles removed from his peaceful Mennonite settlement of Nieder-Chortitza in Ukraine. Surely the good Lord would not let it happen here.

"Put the child back into her crib," my mother called from the kitchen. "The soup's getting cold." Anganetha Penner Dyck, my mother, was a practical woman, not given to brooding about the future. Life was to be enjoyed, and she was determined to make the most of it. Wherever she went she was the life of the party. In no time, she'd have a crowd of people around her as she entertained them with her animated stories. With eyes flashing and hands in motion, she'd act out the story holding everyone spellbound. Soon her listeners would dissolve in laughter begging for more.

But it was my father whom I adored. To me he was the most handsome man in the village: his blond hair combed back from a high intelligent forehead, deep-set eyes crested by dark eyebrows, a faint mustache on lips curled in a smile. I have only one memory of my life in Kronstal, Chortitza, southern Ukraine, and that involves my father. For Christmas he had bought me a doll, the kind every young girl wanted: a doll with a porcelain face and eyes that opened and closed. One day I was playing with my doll near our white picket fence by the road. Carefully I dressed her in underwear, a slip, and a dress. Then I wrapped a warm blanket around her, just as I'd seen my mother do with my baby brothers, Henry and Peter. Three boys stopped by the fence and watched me play with her.

"Show us your doll," the biggest boy said.

I unwrapped the doll and raised her higher so he could take a better look at her. In a flash, he grabbed my doll, tearing her from my hands. "Let's go, " he yelled. They ran down the street, my doll dangling from the boy's fist.

"Give me back my doll," I called. The boy turned around, made a face at me, then disappeared around the corner. I ran along the fence to the edge of our garden, yelling and crying, but the boys did not come back. When my father came home from work, I told him about my lost doll.

"Let's go look for her," my father said, "The boys may have dropped her by the road." He took my small hand in his big calloused one, and we walked down the street together. We looked everywhere, among the tall grasses and in the ditches, but we could not find the doll.

"I'll speak to their parents," my father consoled me. But the boys flatly denied any involvement, and my father, a gentle person who did not like to upset the neighbours, dropped the case. I never did see my doll again. Looking back now, it seemed to foreshadow so much of my first thirty-seven years of life when many things I valued dearly were ruthlessly snatched from me.

In 1917, when I was five years old, our family of six (three brothers had joined us by then: Henry, Peter, and Gerhard) moved to Nieder-Chortitza. It was a beautiful village of 3,000 inhabitants lying on the west bank of the mighty Dnieper where the river divides into two arms, forming Chortitza Island, and then winds its way south to the Black Sea. My grandparents on my mother's side, Henry and Anganetha Penner, and all my mother's siblings lived there, as well as my father's three brothers, Abraham, Jakob, and Peter, and their families. My parents rented a small adobe house at the far end of the village with a garden that bordered a Russian cemetery. At first my father worked in a factory but when his brother Peter died of typhoid, my father took over the operation of his windmill which stood on a small hill just outside the village.

Some of my happiest childhood memories come from playing near my father's mill. I would watch as horse-drawn wagons, laden with sacks of wheat, rye, or barley came clattering onto the yard. A Russian peasant would help my father hoist the sacks to the second storey. Later my father emptied each sack into a large funnel. When the funnel was full, he'd hurry downstairs to crank a handle which moved two sharp stones across the grain. The flour was caught in a sack attached to a funnel. When the sack was full, he'd remove it and replace it with another sack. It always intrigued me how brown kernels of grain dumped into one chute could come out as white flour from another. My father, his cap and trousers dusted with flour, worked the whole operation by himself. A few days later, the Russian farmers returned with their wagons to claim their sacks of flour.

Every day, my father studied the wind. If the wind was too strong, he would take panels out of the vanes. In a good wind, he'd leave them in. But if there was no wind at all, he would turn the large sails by hand. As I watched him strain at the big wheel, my heart filled with admiration. How strong my father was!

In the summer when he worked long hours, I brought him his lunch and supper. One day my friends and I spied a large wheat field on the way to the windmill. The stalks, several feet high, bore swollen heads, almost ready for harvesting. *Perfect for playing hide and seek,* we thought. The chase began. Whooping and laughing, we ducked in and out of the tall wheat, the prickly ears scratching my face. Suddenly I heard my father's whistle. His face was red and unusually serious. "Children, you've trampled down a farmer's wheat field," he said angrily. "He'll have a hard time harvesting his grain now." Then he turned to me, "You're the oldest, Neta, I expect more from you." I looked down at my feet. How I hated to disappoint my father!

My father was a strict disciplinarian tapered by much kindness. One day Tante Lentje came from Neuendorf for a visit. Henry and I played quietly in the bedroom while the adults ate their meal of *zwieback* (buns) and *borscht* (cabbage soup) in the adjoining living room. All morning I had sniffed the delicious aroma of buns baking and cabbage simmering in beef broth flavoured with tomatoes and dill. *I hope they'll leave something for me,* I thought. In those days, polite decorum dictated that children stay out of the way of visitors and eat their meal after the adults had finished. As usual, I heard Mother's animated talking followed by joyous laughter. I wondered how it happened that wherever my mother was, people had a good time. Finally, it was time for us children to eat. Mother called Henry and me to come to the table and placed two bowls of steaming soup before us. I had just about finished my meal, when I heard Tante Lentje saying that she wanted to go for a walk to the Dnieper River.

"I want to come too," I said.

"First a nap, then you may go," my mother said.

As I lay in bed, I worried, *what if they go without me?* Well, I wouldn't let that happen.

I forced myself to stay awake, but despite myself, I fell asleep.

An hour later I awoke. The house was empty. I bolted from the house and looked down the street. Nothing. Frantic now, I ran past the cemetery, past the woods, and up a hill. Totally out of breath, I caught up with them by the windmill. My mother turned around and began to scold me.

"Don't scold her," my aunt said. "You *did* promise her."

My father gently hoisted me onto his back and carried me piggyback the rest of the way to the Dnieper River. Since my brothers, Henry, Peter and Gerhard, who was a baby, were still sleeping at home, I don't think we stayed away long.

Our Home On Soviet Street

A couple of years after we moved to Nieder-Chortitza, the soviet government subdivided a piece of land near the Dnieper and divided the lots among people who owned no land. Our family received an half-hectare (one and a quarter acres) and my father built a sod house with an adjoining barn on it. Our house had three rooms clustered around a large, brick, grass-burning oven: a living room (Grosse Stube), a bedroom (Kleine Stube), and a kitchen. In a small pantry beside the kitchen was a trapdoor which led to a root cellar below. The central oven's two vents could be opened for added warmth. In the chimney slabs of ham, bacon, and sausages were hung to be smoked to a perfect flavour. On a platform inside the oven, Mother cooked and baked all our meals in winter. There was also a small compartment in the brickwork to one side of the fire which kept food warm for a long time. Twice a day, a fire was lit and I, as the oldest child, kept feeding it with handfuls of straw, or maize cobs, or sunflower stalks. On Sundays and holidays we used bricks of dried cow dung which didn't burn up so rapidly and kept the heat longer. During warmer weather when the oven was not fired up, my mother prepared our food on a stove in the kitchen. And in summer she used an adobe stove in the backyard to keep the house cool.

The side of the brick oven in the living room was covered with smooth, glazed tiles, making a comfortable, warm place to lean against after the fire had died down. On winter evenings, my father would sit in the fading daylight on a bench, lean against the oven for warmth, and sing hymns or folk songs in his rich baritone voice. We children would crowd around him and sing along. I can still remember some of the songs he taught me so many years ago.

After the kerosene lamp was lit, and supper dishes were cleared away, my father would ask me to take a book from the shelf and bring it to him. As he read to us children about faraway places, I would hang onto his every word, basking in the wonder of Christmas trees growing in forests and oceans of water much wider than our Dnieper River. Other times, I would ask him to tell me, again, about the "old times," when great grandfather had come to this country on the back of a wagon. "They left everything behind in Prussia, except what they could carry on a wagon," my father would say. "They were seeking a country where they could freely practice their beliefs." Father would show me a yellowed, black and white photo of the first sod home with a straw roof his grandfather had built on a small piece of land in Nieder-Chortitza. How I loved these times with Father! But all too soon the big Kröger clock on the wall announced bedtime. My mother would open two sleep-benches, secure the lid to the back of the bench, pull out a drawer filled with straw, and proceed to make our beds. Two children slept in each bench. In the morning, the process was reversed and our beds became benches again. All the blankets and pillows were piled onto my parents' bed in the Kleine Stube, covered with a bedspread, and topped with two decorative pillows. A high bed was a status symbol: the higher the bed, the richer the people!

Ukrainian summers were hot. When temperatures hovered in the eighties and nineties, my mother cooked our meals on an adobe stove in the backyard. When the meal was ready, we'd gather 'round a picnic table in the shade of an elm tree. Nearby ran a path to the river, and a steady stream of young swimmers hurried across to the beach. After finishing my meal, I'd sometimes join the children in their fun as they swam in the warm water or collected sea shells on its sandy shore. But often my interest was diverted to the sandy ridges sprinkled with tufts of coarse grass and pink, red, and white flowers and purple thyme. I'd hoe among the plants and water them with a little pail. My mother grumbled about it being a waste of time to work among wildflowers, but my father would wink at me and say, "Never mind, I enjoy the flowers too."

Because our yard was so near the shore of the Dnieper, the soil was too sandy to grow an orchard and vegetable garden, as most people had, but we did grow beautiful watermelons and sunflowers, provided we had sufficient rain.

Since we didn't have modern conveniences, much family activity centred around daily living chores, and I, being the oldest, was often called upon to help with scrubbing laundry at the Dnieper or hauling water for our baths, milking the cow twice a day and feeding her newborn calf. My father also needed me to help him with the harvesting. My small arms hardly reached around a sheaf, but I tried very hard to tie them as my father did. During harvest, I carried large melons up to the attic and placed them amidst piles of wheat and shelled corn. I also helped my mother make sauerkraut, a variety of pickles, canned tomatoes, and watermelon syrup. To prepare for winter, we buried carrots in sand and stored potatoes in sacks in the cellar. Small pears which grandmother gave us were dried in the sun.

In October or November, our family spent two happy days at grandmother's place butchering, first her pig and then ours. After butchering, the pig was scalded in a large cauldron. Then it was eviscerated and cut up; liver sausages and farmer sausages were made; lard was rendered; and hams were prepared for smoking. There was a job for everyone. While all this work was going on, people talked and joked. One trick the boys liked to play on the girls was to pin the pig's tail onto somebody's backside. A lot of snickering usually gave the game away. When the tail was discovered, it was kept hidden until, at another unguarded moment, it could be pinned onto somebody else. By the end of the day, this happy group of people had produced buckets filled with lard–a good pig was judged by the volume of lard produced—crocks filled with headcheese and crackles; a mound of spareribs and pickled pig's feet, and a ham ready to hang in the large chimney in the house. After cleaning up, everybody sat down to a supper of *borscht* (cabbage soup), baked buns and spareribs. We rejoiced in the abundance of food shared in the company of family and friends.

Nieder-Chortitza, was a quiet, rural village where everybody knew everybody else. Whether butchering a pig, plowing the fields in spring, or bringing in the harvest in the fall, it was a community effort. If there was an accident or a barn burned down, people rallied around to help. People would drop in for a visit without waiting for an invitation. That was the custom then. If you met someone on the street, you would greet each other and stop to chat. To walk past without saying hello was considered very rude. Everyone took pride in keeping yards and fields tidy. White picket fences hemmed in tidy gardens and orchards. On a spring day, when I came down a hill by the entrenchments, the view almost took my breath away. Blooming acacia trees lined the streets, their fragrance filling the air. Neat rows of small houses ended at the shore, the wide expanse of the river glistened in the sunlight, and on the far shore lay the city of Zaporozhye formerly known as Alexandrowsk. An island, long and narrow, parted the waters at one end of the river. *Nieder-Chortitza is the most beautiful place on earth,* I would think. None of us knew, of course, how soon this peaceful community would be ravaged by political unrest and anarchy.

Troubled Times: Bandits, Typhus, Inflation and Famine

I was just two years old when World War I (1914-1917) broke out and German soldiers marched into our Mennonite villages. Now the Russians who had always been friendly toward us began to distrust us because we were German. We were not allowed to write letters to Germany or to America. Any letters that did get through to us were quickly destroyed. Within all of Russia there was much revolutionary unrest fuelled by the writings of Lenin. He called for an end to the war, for government ownership of all land, and for the overthrow of the czarist government.

Not having a radio we had limited news of the outside world. Our village received one newspaper a month, called *"Pravda,"* meaning "truth." We felt the news was slanted and often outdated. So we got our real news from travellers or itinerant preachers.

The news that Czar Nicholas II was deposed came first to the city of Zaporozhye. Soon it spread to every village. The *schulze* (mayor) of Nieder-Chortitza called together representatives from every home. "You must remove every photo of the czar from your houses," he said. (It was customary for every home to have a large photo of the czar on the wall.) That day in March 1917 was a sad one for us. Life had been good under the czar's regime; we were afraid of Lenin's drastic measures.

A few months later, in October 1917, Russia was torn by civil war (1918-1920) between the Red Army (the communist Bolsheviks) and the White Army (representing the old regime). The Red Army worked to overturn the czarist government and to put power in the hands of the people. Their simple slogan was: "Bread, peace, land." This had real meaning to starving families, soldiers sick of war, and peasants and factory workers tired of corrupt landlords. So, they largely supported the Reds. The Whites supported the old regime. They were poorly organized and the Reds defeated them. In 1922 the Union of Soviet Socialist Republics of Russia (USSR) was established with Lenin as ruler and Joseph Stalin as general secretary of the Communist Party.

During this time of political instability, before the communists had their government firmly in place, groups of bandits on horseback thundered into Mennonite villages plundering homes, burning down barns, raping women, and often killing their husbands. The most notorious leader was Nestor Makhno. For some reason, he had a personal grudge against Mennonites. During one night in October, 1919, he and his bandits stormed into every home of Eichenfeld and killed all the males, 81 in total.

To protect their families and themselves against these attacks, men from the settlements banded together to form a self defence unit *(selbstschutz)*. In our village ten men volunteered. They took turns standing at the entrance of Nieder-Chortitza with guns in hand to chase away the bandits.(German soldiers going home after World War I had given them the guns). The Mennonite Church, firmly believing in and teaching pacifism, was very much against this. Yet the men felt it was their obligation to protect the women and children. But they were no match for Machno's men. In fact, once their names were known to the bandits, they were put on Machno's hit list. My uncle Abraham who'd joined the selbstschutz had gone into hiding. To protect his family from the bandits his wife, aunt Mary, and their three children had moved into my maternal grandmother's home. One very cold winter day, uncle Abraham came home. Hearing the bandits had entered the village, he escaped to the hayloft. The bandits searched the house and took anything of value,

11

then they headed for the barn. They found uncle Abraham under a pile of straw and killed him. Then they tossed his body out of the hayloft onto the yard below. Aunt Mary never recovered from the shock of her husband's murder.

We lived in constant fear of the bandits. On any given day, these ragged men would barge into our homes and take whatever they fancied. Once a bandit found my father's black suit which my mother kept hidden in the sleep-bench under the straw. He slung it over his shoulder and made for the door. My mother, a feisty woman, wasn't about to stand there while her husband's best and only suit walked away. She grabbed it and whisked it off the bandit's shoulder. He whirled around and whipped her back. Undaunted, she snarled, "Get out of my house." Surprisingly, the bandit left and my mother was able to keep the suit.

Late one evening, as I was lying in my sleep-bench, I heard a loud pounding on the outside door. Cautiously, my mother opened it, and two bandits pushed in. "Fix this for us," one barked, as he handed my mother a chicken, its feet tied with a vine.

"Neta, come make a fire," my mother called.

When the water was hot, my mother scalded the chicken, and I helped her pull off the feathers. As the chicken roasted, I fed the fire with smaller handfuls of straw. Out of the corner of my eye, I kept watching our strange company. Their clothes smelled, their hair was matted, they had bloodshot eyes and they were rude and impatient. I kept wishing my father were home, but he was working extra late at the mill. When the meal was ready, the bandits hungrily devoured the roasted chicken and then they left.

Another time, my mother saw two bandits plundering a home across the street. Quickly she closed the draft on the cookstove and black smoke began to pour into the kitchen. When the bandits entered our house, they couldn't see for the smoke; they cursed my mother, then turned on their heels and left. I don't remember being unduly frightened of these strange men. I think my mother's courage and take-charge attitude helped me feel secure.

The bandits also stormed my father's windmill. They would stick their swords into the sacks of grain and rip them open, spilling the grain onto the floor. But they never found money or some hoped-for hidden treasure and eventually they left him alone.

Once the civil war was over and a government was in place, Nestor Machno was exiled and the raids stopped. But the government could not stop the dreaded typhus fever from entering our homes. This deadly plague had been carried from house to house by the lice crawling on the heads and filthy clothes of the bandits. At my maternal grandmother's home, everyone became violently ill. My grandfather and uncle Peter and uncle Henry died. Soon my father, also, showed the dreaded symptoms of headache, chills, extreme high fever, and general pains. Thank God, my mother remained healthy and strong; she nursed my father, and helped my grandmother as much as she could. Miraculously, none of us children became ill. Every day more people died. A few strong men dug graves but they could not keep up with the demand. Now family graves were left open so that all the dead people from one family could be buried in one grave. During those dreadful months of winter 1919-1920 a total of 94 people died in our small village of Nieder-Chortitza. Of course, there weren't enough coffins and they, too, had to be shared. My father survived, but his recovery was slow. For many days, he was too weak to walk by himself.

After the Revolution the currency changed to Red money. The old money with the czar's image on it wasn't worth anything anymore. You couldn't even trade it in for

Red money. My father, along with everyone else, lost all their money. One box of matches cost 1,000,000 rubles, one pound of butter cost 5,000,000 rubles, Red money. Soon we could not buy even the most basic needs, like kerosene for our lamps or matches to light fires. Mother placed a small saucer of sunflower oil on the top of a dresser with a piece of wool yarn in it. She would light the yarn with a burning stick from the fire. This gave us a small light. We didn't dare put our precious light on the table for fear somebody would breathe too hard and blow it out.

When our fuel was gone, we hunted along the shore of the frozen Dnieper for scrub among the willows. Although the sticks we brought home were often green, my father would coax them into burning. The fire hissed and sizzled as drops of sap fell into the flames. On some mornings, the fire was completely out. Then my father would summon me out of my bed.

"Neta, come to the window," my father called. "See if there's smoke somewhere."

As my bare feet hit the cold loam floor, I shivered. Hurriedly I dressed and joined my father at the frozen windowpane. I drew in a deep breath, then blew on the glass until a peep hole formed among the ice-ferns. I strained my eyes to find a wisp of smoke curling from a neighbour's chimney.

"I see smoke—by Penner's," I said.

"Quickly get dressed and get us some fire," my father said.

I pulled on my winter coat, put my feet into wooden slippers, grabbed a pot, and ran to the neighbour's house to borrow a few glowing embers. On the way home, I walked very slowly so the coals wouldn't die. Father placed the precious embers among a handful of straw and blew on them until an acrid smoke burst into a small flame. Then he added small twigs and blew again. The fire smoked and sizzled as timid flames licked at the green twigs. Eventually, a new fire burned brightly and we gathered around its homey warmth.

When I was seven, I started school in a nice building not far from our home where grades 1-4 were taught. The official language of instruction was high-German. At home we spoke a dialect, called low-German or *platt deutsch*. But this was no problem for me, for our church services were also conducted in high-German. My entire school supplies consisted of an old slate, a slate pencil, and a nice pencil case which my father had made for me. One could not buy writing paper, pencils, or books. Teachers taught orally and wrote on a blackboard on the wall. They drilled us in writing until it became an art: each letter neatly carved onto the slate. For Christmas, we were each given a sheet of paper on which we copied poems written out in our best handwriting and illustrated with drawings. These were our "Christmas cards." We recited the poems on Christmas morning to our parents.

During my first year of school, I had a Mennonite teacher who started the day with a hymn and prayer. But the second year, the government sent a communist teacher who taught us that there is no God and that the Bible is full of fairy tales. Instead of a hymn, we began the day with the communist national anthem. In another song we sang, *The aeroplanes soared higher and higher into the sky and they have never seen God.* "There is no God," he said. "Our help comes from Lenin and communism." He painted a picture of Russia so grand that it sounded like we'd be living in a paradise where no one was hungry anymore and everyone was treated equal. It's no wonder that some children joined the Pioneers—young communists-in-training. They wore a red tie and received preferential treatment.

A Christmas To Remember

Because there was no church building in town, worship services were conducted in the school building. On Saturday, the portable walls separating two classrooms would be removed, creating a room big enough for the congregation. Of course, we had no piano. Three choristers, called *vorsänger*, would begin to sing a hymn and soon everybody in the congregation chimed in, sounding like a choir of four-part harmony. My school teacher, Hans Rempel, was also our preacher.

During the festive season, people did their best to lay cares and worries aside to make Christmas a happy occasion. I'll never forget these wonderful times. On Christmas Eve, after our baths, we dressed in our best and warmest clothes, then joined the crowd walking to the school building for the traditional Christmas Eve program. Inside, we took our respective places on the benches–men on the right, women and small children on the left. The air was fragrant with the smell of a large evergreen tree up front, the only Christmas tree in the village. After the singing and recitations by school children, the most wonderful moment arrived: the lighting of the Christmas tree. Two men, carrying long sticks with lighted candles, walked to the front of the room and lit the candles on the tree, one by one, until the whole tree began to glitter and shine. In the soft, flickering candle light the vorsängers began to sing, "Silent Night, Holy Night," and everyone chimed in–sopranos, altos, tenors, and basses.

Back at home, before going to bed, each of us children placed a dinner plate on a table in the Grosse Stube for Weihnachtsmann (Santa) to fill. But on Christmas Eve, 1921, the year I was nine, my father sadly announced, "Children, there will be no gifts this year."

Ukraine, along with the rest of Russia, was in the grip of a severe famine. Russia had suffered six and a half years of wars (World War I followed by the Russian Revolution). Along with the ravages of war, the weather played havoc with the crops. For weeks hot winds blew relentlessly across the fields. What little there was to be harvested, Machno bandits took for themselves. There was no harvest and no food in the stores. Many people died of starvation. Many more would have died had the Mennonite Central Committee (MCC) not sent help from America. School children received a bowlful of rice and a piece of white bread for lunch. Some days we even got a cup of hot cocoa. At an MCC soup kitchen poor families received one meal a day. Yes, times were harsh; we children knew that. Still, it was Christmas, and we expected Santa to surmount these odds.

"Children, you have already received a most wonderful gift," my father continued. "A baby sister!" Our faces fell. True, four days ago while we were sleeping at grandmother's house, Tina, my sister was born. After three brothers, I was thrilled to have a baby sister, but surely Santa didn't think this was all that we children wanted.

Christmas morning I awakened early. Dutifully I stood before my father and mother sitting on the bench in the Grosse Stube, folded my hands and began to recite my poem:

"Nun ist sie da die schöne Stunde,	(now has arrived the happy time)
auf die sich alle Kinder freuen	(which all children were waiting for)
Tief bewegt mit Herz und Munde	(with joyful hearts and glad voices)
dem Eltern ihre Wünsche weihen."	(to speak a blessing to their parents)

There were more stanzas, but I can't remember them now, except that I wished my parents health, a long life, and happiness. Next my brothers said their wishes, thankfully shorter than mine, for the older you were the longer your poem had to be. This out of the way, we dashed into the Grosse Stube to check on our plates. Sure enough, Santa had left us a gift: three rye cakes lay in each plate.

Easter Celebration

In March the ice on the Dnieper River, which had been our skating rink all winter, began to crack and rumble. We would run to the shore to watch the ice floes pile up into craggy mountains that glistened in the sunshine as they drifted slowly down river. In a few days, small boats ferried people from Nieder-Chortitza to the city of Zaporozhye. Most often, by Easter, the snow and ice was gone. The whole yard was raked and swept so everything would be clean and festive. During better days, my mother would bake the familiar Easter bread (*paska*) and plan the Easter meal of ham and *ploomamoos* (a fruit soup). Meanwhile, my father would prepare a surprise for us. Weeks before, in a rusty, old dish pan he'd seed some rye, and, by Easter time, the shoots were several inches high. Among this delicate greenery, he'd place coloured Easter eggs. Of course, there was no food colouring to buy, but, being an artist at heart, my father had invented his own food colouring: boiled moss for green, onion skins for yellow, a bleeding red fabric for red, a drop of ink for blue.

But on Easter 1922, there were no colourful eggs hidden among rye shoots, no sweet Easter bread, or festive meal. Although Santa had managed to make it for Christmas, there were no surprises for Easter. Even the MCC soup kitchen in town had dried up for the communists had stopped all foreign aid. They didn't see the need for it, even though people were starving.

But there was still one place where my brothers hoped to find a little food. In Rasumowka, a neighbouring village, Russian peasants would be bringing food to the graveyard in honour of their departed loved ones. The priest would bless the food, and then it would be distributed among the children. My brothers planned to be there to get some food. And so did I, except that I was shivering with malaria fever. But the lure of food was strong. As Henry and Peter prepared to go, I begged my parents to let me go too.

"You're sick, Neta," my mother said.

"I feel better," I lied. For weeks I had dreamed about eating a piece of Easter bread or a hard boiled egg; I simply couldn't stay home.

Finally, my parents gave in to my pleading.

Despite my best intentions not to be a nuisance to my brothers, I couldn't keep up with them. My fever persisted and my head ached. My feet felt like lead as I stumbled along. It wasn't far, but the Dnieper had flooded, necessitating a big detour. Finally, my brothers each grabbed my hand and pulled me along. When we arrived at the graveyard, I dropped onto the nearest grave, closed my eyes, and lay there shivering with fever. "Neta, get up," I heard my father calling. Was I dreaming? No, as I opened my eyes, I looked into the tender blue eyes of my father. Being worried about me, he had followed us to Rasumowka. Under a tree, he spread out his jacket and invited me to lie down on it. I did, and soon I fell sound asleep. When I awoke, my father offered me some fruit soup. I looked at him wide-eyed. Where did my father find such a treat? Hungrily, I ate most of it. Then I fell asleep again. When I awoke, the gravestones cast long shadows across the quiet graveyard. Most of the people had gone home, including my brothers.

"My headache's gone," I said.

"Good," my father smiled. "Let's go home then."

Many people in our village suffered with malaria and they usually treated it with quinine. But I'm certain, the fruit soup so lovingly offered by my father did more for my malaria than any medication would have done.

While Russian peasants clung to their traditions, the communists did their best to discredit religion. In schools and at compulsory public meetings, they preached that "religion is the opiate of the people." Teachers came from the city to indoctrinate us school children. They mocked table grace or prayers before going to bed. "God is a myth and the Bible is a book of fairy tales," they said. "Only fools believe in God." Soon their tactics became more severe. They forbad public meetings altogether. Our small congregation left the public school house and moved into the Siemen's granary. Since religion classes were cancelled in school, they were now offered in the granary, but quietly and very discreetly lest the communist authorities find out about them

After completing grade three, I did not return to school. My mother needed full-time help with her growing family of seven, and it was customary for the oldest girl to help out in this way. Still, I was heart broken to give up my formal education. But my father consoled me, "In the evening, you will read to me by the fire," he said. "That way you will get sufficient practice in reading. And when you grow up, you can become a good seamstress like Tante Lentje in Neuendorf."

Heavy Work For A Ten-year Old

My chores as a ten-year old were many: I washed all the diapers and most of the family laundry by hand. In summer, I washed them in the Dnieper, and in the winter, in a tub in the kitchen. Very early in the morning, I milked the cow, but sometimes, as I leaned into the cow's warm belly, I fell asleep. Suddenly, I'd be startled awake by the horn of the village herdsman sounding very near. If I missed him, I would have the added chore of taking the cow to the communal pasture myself. My small hands flew as I finished milking; then I quickly untied the cow, and let her join the herd as it passed our gate. In the evening I would darn or knit socks. I also helped my father and mother harvest and prepare food for winter. Often when I was feeding the fire, I would sneak a book from my father's bookshelf and soon I was so engrossed in reading, that I would let the fire go out. My mother's scolding never cured me of an intense desire to explore the world of learning.

One evening, my Uncle Peter Dyck, who was married to my mother's sister, became violently ill. Was the dreaded typhus back? Nobody knew, but to be safe, he was kept in isolation in his bedroom. When Uncle Peter called out for water, nobody wanted to go in. Finally, I couldn't stand his agonized pleas anymore. I snuck in the back door and hurried to his bedside. I held a glass of water to his mouth and watched him gulp it down. The next day, Uncle Peter died. Soon four pallbearers carried my uncle's bed out of the house, his lifeless body covered with a sheet, and proceeded to walk to the cemetery. *Are they really going to bury Uncle Peter in his bed?* I wondered. Curious, my cousins and I joined the small procession to the cemetery. As I watched them lower the bed into a grave, I shuddered. *What a dreadful sickness!* A health inspector from Zaporozhye was summoned. After a brief investigation, he concluded my uncle had died of cholera. He placed a black flag on the roof putting the house under quarantine.

Meanwhile, Aunt Tina and my two cousins were stuck in the contaminated house. Nobody dared go in to them except my grandmother. She was a small woman with a big heart ready to welcome people in need. Tante Anna, my mother's sister who was single, lived with her, as did Aunt Mary, Uncle Abraham's widow, with her three children, and Uncle Gerhard, grandmother's brother-in-law. Now she invited Aunt Tina and her children to come live with her. I wondered how so many people could live in such a small house, but somehow my grandmother always found room.

Our worship services in the Siemen's granary carried on sporadically for the next two years. Sunday school was usually held on Sunday afternoons. When I was about twelve, I learned a part in a church drama called "The good voice versus the bad voice." The voice of atheistic propaganda was becoming increasingly louder. I believe our church leaders were trying to encourage us to listen to the still small Voice within.

During the next four years, more and more religious freedom was taken away from us. Eventually, all religious gatherings were forbidden. Our worship services in the granary ceased. Many pastors and their families were sent to Siberia. Despite the danger, Aaron Toews, a man of courage walked from village to village to encourage the believers. News of his arrival would be whispered about and people would gather at an appointed meeting place.

CHAPTER TWO

My Youth: At Odds with Communist Ideology

ONE NIGHT IN 1924, when I was twelve, I was awakened by sirens blaring all night. The urgent sound echoed across the water from a city on the other side of the river. I jumped out of bed and joined the others in the kitchen. In the distance we saw lights in the factories. What was happening? We didn't know but it must be something important. In the morning, my father went to enquire and came back with the news, "Lenin has died."

After Lenin's death, Leon Trotsky came into power and he was eager to implement full socialism in Russia. Now the communist government took land from the rich and divided it among the poor, two hectares per person (about five acres). Suddenly our family of eight owned a large field of 39.5 acres outside the village west of Nieder-Chortitza. My father bought two horses, one cow, a pig, a few chickens, and a wagon. He built a small shelter for our animals. Besides a few hoes and rakes, we had no farm implements. All we had was a rickety, old wagon pulled by two horses: a large brown horse and a much smaller, reddish-coloured horse.

Since my father still worked at the Friesen's gristmill (our windmill had been destroyed in a bad storm) and my mother was busy with housework and minding her youngest two children—Gerhard (7 years old) and Tina (4 years old)—the work in the fields was done by us older children: Peter (9 years old), Henry (11 years old), and me (12 years old).

Sometimes, as we passed a wagon with a handsome team of horses, people pointed at us and laughed, "Look at that big horse harnessed to a small horse," someone would say, "some farmers they are!" My cheeks flushed and I felt like shouting, "We may not have the best team of horses, but you should see how clean we keep our fields!" But of course, I said nothing. I took great pride in hoeing among the melon plants until not a weed remained. We had a good harvest that fall and some days Henry hauled away three wagon-loads of the sweetest watermelons to the ferry. They were sold at a market in the city or in a Russian village.

In the fall, my father took us to Zaporozhye to go shopping for shoes and clothes. We always bought shoes several sizes too big so that they would last for a few years. Leather shoes were worn on Sundays only; the rest of the time, we wore wooden slippers. My father also bought me a brand new coat and two pieces of wool fabric which Tante Lentje sewed into two beautiful dresses for me. When I surveyed my wonderful wardrobe, I felt incredibly lucky. I'd never owned that many clothes before.

My Youth Group

During my early teens, seven of us girls spent a lot of time together. Most often we met in my grandmother's garden. We played games or we sang for hours with Tante Anna accompanying us on her guitar. On a Sunday summer afternoon, when we weren't swimming in the Dnieper, we would stroll on the shore of the river, walking barefoot on the warm sand, and collect beautiful sea shells. Sometimes a girl in the group had brought along some roasted sunflower seeds tied in a hanky. As she shared them with us, we'd sit on the large rocks by the shore and crack the seeds between our teeth and spit them out, splattering the white sand. While ferries and ships plowed the waters, we whiled away the hours, laughing and talking. None of us owned a watch, but suddenly someone would say, "chore time," and we'd all hurry home.

As we grew older, boys sometimes joined us. On warm evenings, we would congregate in someone's garden and play games that evoked a lot of laughter and teasing. Or we'd have a good-old fashioned singsong. Sometimes my brothers, Henry and Peter, accompanied us on the mandolin and balalaika. How I loved these carefree, fun-filled evenings! Often, when I went to bed at night, I'd go to sleep with the sound of singing in the distance. Russian field hands who lived in our village would sing their beautiful folk songs until the early morning hours.

In the spring of 1926, my sister Annie was born. She must have been a good baby because I can't remember any naughty episodes. She was a beautiful child with straw-coloured hair and sky-blue eyes. My six-year-old sister, Tina, played with her for hours on end, but at fourteen, I had little time to spend with my baby sister. Perhaps this is why I have so few memories of her. Two years later, our family was blessed with another baby brother. Hans was a beautiful, intelligent child who quickly became everyone's darling. Sadly, he lived only three years.

A Great Loss

After his bout with typhus, my father's health declined. Eventually, he quit his job at the Friesen's mill and stayed home altogether. He began to spend more and more time in bed. The doctors in Chortitza were puzzled by his illness and did not know how to help him.

Wanting to cheer up my father, I would pick him a bouquet of wildflowers on our way home from the field. At the sight of them, his eyes always lit up in his thin, pale face. In the spring of 1929, my father felt strong enough to come to the field with us to help us plant tomatoes. But often he stopped to rest, leaning on a hoe. As he scanned the field, I heard him say, "I won't live long enough to harvest these tomatoes." Shocked, I turned away, not wanting to hear more; I could not imagine life without my father. But as I watched him push away his meals and losing weight, I worried. *What can I do to bring a little nourishment to him?* I remembered my father saying he liked a particular soft drink. I hurried to the ferry dock and waited for a shipment to come in from Zaporozhye. I bought a bottle and took it home to him. He took a few sips, then pushed it away. "It hurts my stomach," he said. Even the little food he did eat wouldn't stay down.

Still, my father did not complain. He would call us to his bedside and request that we sing one of his favourite hymns. He'd hum the tune or mouth the words along with us. Or he'd ask me to read a well-worn Scripture portion from his Bible. But the time came when even this was too much effort for his pain-racked body. At night, his anguished screams awakened me. In my nightgown, I'd flee from the house, hide behind a big straw pile, and sob.

In August 1929, my father died.

My father's funeral was conducted in the Siemen's granary. It was a Mennonite custom to have an open casket and to take one last photo of the family around the coffin. As we filed past, I stared at my father's lifeless form: eyes tightly closed, lips drawn in a tight line, blond hair slicked back from his forehead. I wanted him to open his blue eyes. I wanted his mouth to form in a shy smile. I wanted him to say, "It's all a mistake. I'm alright." But he lay motionless, his black tie neatly tucked under his white shirt collar. People said things like, "Doesn't he look peaceful?" "Why did he have to die so young?" "He's in a better place." None of it was a comfort to me. At seventeen I needed my father–now. How could life go on without him?

Throughout the long months when my father was so critically ill, I had avoided my friends.

I had stayed away from the youth gatherings in grandmother's garden. I didn't want to sing songs or play games when my father was dying. Following the funeral, I shrank from company even more. The one person who'd loved me most in the world was gone. Yes, I still had my mother, but with her no-nonsense approach to life, she had no patience for tears. Her attitude seemed to be: life is tough, so get used to it! With the breadwinner gone, life for our family became an intense struggle for survival. I think the only way my mother could cope at all, was to distance herself from the pain. But in this way, she also distanced herself from her children. Often I felt very much alone and misunderstood. In time, though, I found courage to return to my youth group. Yet it wasn't the same group I had left some months ago. Many of my friends had immigrated to Canada; some had been banished to Siberia. Only Aaron Toews, the itinerant preacher from Chortitza, remained. He walked from village to village, in summer and winter, to serve us the Word of God.

I Work in a Kolkhoz

Stalin's power in the Communist Party grew rapidly and in December, 1927, he won a sweeping victory. He removed his rivals from power and became dictator of the Soviet Union. Now times became very bad for us. Lenin and Trotsky had introduced the socialist program with its two major goals: First, the small peasant farms would be combined into government controlled *kolkhoz* (collective farms). Second, the production of heavy industry would be expanded.

Stalin ruled by terror. He'd given himself the name Stalin, Russian for "man of steel," and it suited him well. Being in a hurry to implement his five-year plans to expand Russia's economy, he put severe pressure on all farmers to unite and work their land collectively. Estate owners were accused of being *kulaks* (tightfisted ones) and enemies of the state. At the beginning of 1929 the kulaks began to be heavily taxed, then they were evicted from their land altogether and deported to unknown destinations. Most were taken to Siberia from where they never returned. Their property became government-controlled farms. Pressure to unite was put on the small farmers as well. Speeches were made to prove that a classless society (a society without rich or poor people) was infinitely better than the old one of free enterprise (privately owned and controlled business). A communist spokesman visited our village and painted a rosy picture of what life on a collective farm would be like. "You'll be able to eat whatever you want—black bread, white bread, cake–you name it. When you need a new dress, you'll be able to enter a store and select the one you want. You see, we'll be sharing everything."

Naturally, the farmers were not convinced. They knew these were empty promises. They remained steadfast in their opposition until Stalin devised a heinous plan that broke even the strongest of them: he instigated a terrible famine in which nearly ten million peasants died. At the end, everything was collectivized—lands, animals, machinery. There was no more opposition.

One day, a government official came to our house and told us that our land, horses, cow, and wagon were now state-owned. What the communists had given us a few years before, they now took away. Many of our friends suffered a worse fate than we did. Their homes were snatched from them and used for the state. Confiscated homes became farm brigade office buildings, day care centres, or communal kitchens where kolkhoz workers received one meal a day.

Like every able-bodied person, I joined a brigade, a compulsory work unit, overseen by a *komsomol* (brigadier). Nobody was exempt. Mothers brought their small children to the day care centres to be cared for while they worked. Children as young as 12 years of age were sometimes conscripted. Each morning the brigadier assigned the work we were to do that day: men to run the machinery; women and girls to hoe the fields or load the wagons. We worked seven days a week. We did not receive a regular wage. Instead, records were kept of how many days each person worked, and at the end of the harvest season, the workers were paid in produce for the whole year's labour. First, the state took its quota; the remainder was divided among the workers. The wage was calculated in this way: for each day a person worked, he received 100 grams of wheat. That's less than a pound a day! Multiply that by the number of days worked, and that was the salary for the year. For example, if a person had worked 365 days in one year, he would receive 36,500 grams of wheat which was 36 ½ kilo (80 pounds). So the worker brought home his salary for the entire year in one sack. If anyone dared to complain, the brigadier would say, "You didn't work hard enough."

My Baptism: Taking A Stand

I was nearly 19 when I was baptized. Being raised in the Mennonite faith, baptism was a big step. It meant taking ownership of one's faith. And in these days, when all loyalty was supposed to be to the state, it was a dangerous thing to do. Aaron Toews, the pastor who instructed us, risked the disapproval of the state to teach us. For six weeks every Sunday morning, I joined a group of young people walking through fields and pasture lands to the church in Burwalde. We walked barefoot to save wear and tear on our shoes, since we couldn't afford to replace them. At the outskirts of the village, we put on our stockings and shoes so we could enter the village looking respectful.

On Pentecost Sunday, 1931, the day of our baptism, winds gusted and dark, menacing clouds rumbled as we ducked into the church for cover. During the service, the storm broke. Meanwhile, thirty candidates, sitting in the front row all dressed in black, strained to hear Pastor Aaron Toews' address, but it was almost impossible to hear above the thunder and the deluge. After a prayer, he invited all candidates to kneel at the altar. He gave each person a special Scripture verse. I still remember mine 65 years later; it was: "Jesus Christ the same yesterday, and today, and forever." (Hebrews 13:8) As I knelt at the altar for my baptism, I made a commitment to follow Jesus no matter what the cost.

When we left the building, a rainbow in vivid colours arched across the sky. *God's special benediction on each of us!* I thought.

To celebrate this important day, all the baptismal candidates were served a lunch of pudding, fried potatoes and bread. I stared at the generous spread and thought, *Where did all this food come from?* Food was still rationed in our homes and this wonderful meal was a costly sacrifice.

At two in the afternoon, we received our church membership, which we celebrated with our first communion. This blessed day remained a shining memory in the dark days ahead when persecution of the church increased. The communists put pressure on Pastor Aaron Toews, offering him a position in government if he would deny his faith, but he refused. So they exiled him to Siberia where he eventually died. Many years later, his daughter in Canada wrote her father's memoir based on the letters he sent her from Siberia. To my delight, I was able to get a copy.

CHAPTER THREE

Stalin's Famine
1932-1933

STALIN'S FIRST FIVE-YEAR plan started in 1928. The government demanded a certain quota and the kolkhoz had to deliver. Often the entire harvest went for export and government reserve stocks used to supply raw materials to industry, to feed the people of the growing manufacturing centres, and to pay for imported machinery. This left nothing for the peasants to take home. When something was left over–after the government had taken its share—it was carefully divided among the workers according to the days they had worked. On those days we might have a little grain or a few potatoes to take home. But many days there was nothing.

Suspecting the people of hoarding produce and selling it on the black market, the communist government instigated house searches. Any food that was found was confiscated. To undermine trust among neighbours, they used Mennonite people to conduct these house searches. One day I was told to search one of our neighbour's homes. "Look in the attic, the cellar and under the bed," I was told, "and report to the authorities if they have stowed away some food." Although I went to the appointed home, I remained standing in the doorway; I felt too embarrassed to go inside and conduct a search. A few days later, a man whom we knew well came to our home and scooped out the last bit of flour from our bin.

"Why are you doing this?" my mother asked him.

"I have no choice," he replied. "Believe me, I'm not doing this of my own free will."

We knew he was telling the truth. Anyone who dared to disobey orders given by the Soviets was shot or banished to Siberia. Neighbour's were encouraged to spy on one another. Then they were summoned for interrogation at night. Severe pressure was put on them to betray one of their own. Demands for money and produce were made, and if the person couldn't deliver, severe punishment followed. This encouraged stealing. We began to be suspicious of our own neighbours. Trust eroded as fear began to take over.

Workers were organized into brigades. I was in the second brigade. Each group of workers had a *komsomol* (a brigadier) who supervised us on horseback. He would crack his whip when he wanted us to work faster. He was always a man; the hard manual work went to the women. That's how it was done in those days. We worked every day, even on Sundays. The brigadier said we could have a day off when it was raining.

After working hard all morning, workers received one bowlful of vegetable soup for lunch. We would gulp it down, hoping for seconds, but there weren't any. We'd return to work with hunger pangs gnawing inside our bellies. Soon all of us lost weight and we became weak and dizzy. Yet we were expected to continue working in the fields. Eventually, I got so weak that I could hardly lift my hoe. At the end of a very long row, I would drop to the ground in exhaustion, like all the other workers did. We would lie there staring up into the blue sky and think about food. Suddenly somebody would shout, "The brigadier!" We'd stagger to our feet, grab our hoes, and begin to swing them again. As usual, he would lecture us on being lazy peasants.

After a very long day, we walked home, often a distance of several kilometres. Appointed watchmen would search the workers before they left the fields. Pockets had to be turned inside out. If caught with a bit of food in the pocket, the punishment was severe. The communists had taught us, "We will share everything. It belongs to all of us anyway." Now, when workers took a handful of grain, or sunflower seeds, or a few potatoes home to their families, the brigadiers called it stealing. A terrible beating followed, or even banishment to Siberia. Once when a friend and I were planting watermelons, a komsomol walked a few paces behind us all day long to make sure we were not eating any seeds. Another day when we were hoeing potatoes, he kept watching us lest we pull up a plant and pick off the small potatoes and eat them. If he hadn't been watching, we would have done so for we were desperately hungry.

Once a komsomol came to our house to interrogate my brother Henry. He had picked up two potatoes the plow had failed to cover and taken them home. Somebody had seen him do it and reported him. In the evening two men came to our home and gave Henry a terrible beating. "Next time, it's Siberia," the communist warned.

Henry was terrified. The next morning, my nineteen-year-old brother was gone. For a long time we did not know where he was. Sometimes people told us they had seen him at the market, but when my mother went to look for him, she never found him. One cold winter day, the door opened a crack and I heard a familiar voice ask, "May I come in?" I dropped my knitting and stared at a haggard person leaning against the door jamb. This dirty, ragged person with matted hair didn't look like my brother, but by his voice I knew it was.

"Come in, Henry!" I cried.

He staggered into the kitchen and dropped onto a chair. "I'm sick," he said weakly.

"Where have you been, Henry?" I asked. "We've been so worried about you."

"I've lived on the streets," he gasped, "but I want to die at home."

You're not going to die, I wanted to say but, looking at my brother's face with its hollow cheeks and sunken eyes, I wasn't at all sure he would make it. He told me he had severe dysentery and was becoming very weak from the loss of blood. "I crawled on my hands and knees to get here," he said.

I called my mother. Like me, she was relieved to see her son again, but also, very worried. "Make him a warm bed in the barn," she told me. I hesitated; did she say *barn?* I wanted my brother to be in the house with the rest of us, but my mother explained, "Dysentery is contagious. We can't risk it." So I fixed a bed on a pile of straw and offered him what little food we had. During the winter months, I kept nursing my brother. My mother was so weak from lack of food that she staggered like a drunk person. *They're both going to die,* I worried. *Oh, God, please help us.*

The answer came in a most surprising and simple way. One day, I answered a knock on the door, and there stood Henry's friend, David Epp, holding a small fish in his hand. "I thought you could cook this for Henry's supper," he said with a smile. I was dumbfounded. David could have easily eaten the fish himself or taken it home to his family. Yet, God had put it on his heart to bring the fish to us. For many weeks thereafter, David shared his catch with our family. Thanks to his friend's generous gifts, my brother's strength increased, little by little, and in the spring he was healthy once more. Then Henry began to forage for food for our family.

One of the best sources of food were field mice. Henry would carry pails of water from the Dnieper to the steppes where the mice lived in burrows. Sometimes Annie, who was too young to work in the kolkhoz, would help him. Henry poured water down the hole flushing out the mice. He'd catch them, kill them, and skin them. On a good day, he'd bring home three mice. Mother would cook a meaty soup adding chopped wild onion, sorrel (a sour-tasting leaf), and lodick (a very big leaf) which Annie had picked in the meadows. On special days, Mother made one pancake for us all to go with the soup.

Stalin used severe famine to get the peasants to cooperate with his collectivization policies. The food situation was better in towns and industrial centres which had a food rationing system. Sometimes Mother sent one of us to Tante Lentje in Neuendorf or to Tante Marie in Chortitza. The thirty kilometre trip on foot was well worth it, for we received a meal and a gift of a few potatoes or beets to take home to Mother.

Our beautiful village lying in the crook of the Dnieper river was changing too. The yards and barns, once so neat and tidy, now lay in shambles. For lack of fuel, people were breaking down their fences. They did it at night, though, for it was against the law.

Mother had long ago taken our prized possessions to the bazaar to barter for food. Our Kröger clock, her sewing machine, and my beautiful Sunday dresses were gone. My father's black suit (the one she saved from the bandits) was also gone. Even so, the return in food was so meagre, it hardly helped stave off hunger. All the cats and dogs in our village were eaten and the field mice became extinct. In the spring, we hunted for wild onions and sorrel and wild berries. We picked the blossoms of acacia trees and cooked them. There simply wasn't any food for us peasants.

And still we had to report to work every day. One day, my work assignment was road construction. How I wished it had been milking cows, for then I could have dipped a hand into the milk pail and sipped a little. Another day, the brigadier ordered us to thresh a pile of straw saying we had not done a good job the first time. But my brigadier was kinder than most. In the evening, after we reported to him, he would leave the barn purposefully so we could help ourselves to a few handfuls of seed. "Girls, don't overdo it," he would call over his shoulder. We knew the risk he was taking—banishment to Siberia if found out–so we tried to be extra careful not to get him into trouble.

We came home in the dark and emptied our pockets of the few seeds or vegetables we had gleaned. Mother cleaned them and cooked them for our supper.

In the mornings I stumbled out of bed and pulled on my work clothes. Mother served us a bowl of soup on which floated bits of wild onions and lodick. Seven-year-old Annie's blue eyes, large as saucers, almost popped out of her pinched, little face as she followed my every spoonful. I could hardly swallow, yet I knew if I gave my breakfast away, I would never make it through another working day.

Annie never whined.

After two years of starvation, my body became so weak that in the evenings after having spent a day in the field, I could hardly make it back to the village. I pulled myself along the picket fence and dragged my unwilling body as far as Grandmother's house. At the gate stood Tante Anna waiting for me with a dried *krushtje* (like crab apple) and a drink of water. That's all she had, but it gave me courage to find the strength to make it home.

In 1933, the weather was good and there was a big crop ready for harvest. The kolkhoz workers who had been starved all year, were so weak that they didn't have the strength to harvest the crop. So the communists brought in factory workers from Zaporozhye to help us. Although the overseers hadn't fed us more than one bowl of vegetable soup a day, now they butchered a cow and cooked a good meaty soup. They also baked bread using some of the harvested rye. People who'd been starved for months dug in with gusty, but their stomachs couldn't handle the food; some became very ill and some even died.

I wasn't in danger of dying from overeating, though, for I couldn't eat at all. Even the smell of the rich soup made me sick. I just lay under the wagon in the shade listening to the others eat. When I got up to work again, I stumbled and fell. The overseer, seeing my condition, sent me home.

My legs were so swollen and heavy that I could hardly lift them. If I fell down, I couldn't get back up again. At bedtime, I would sit on the edge of the bed and wait for my mother to lift my feet into bed so I could lie down. One morning, I was so weak and dizzy, I couldn't get out of bed at all. It was customary to sing hymns for the dying and one night a group of girls came to sing for me. But at twenty-two I wasn't ready to die: I wanted to live. *Dear God, please help me live,* I prayed.

Every two hours, my mother fed me two teaspoons of mashed potatoes with bits of tomato in it. That's all I could tolerate. But I was so thankful for that much! And then, after I got used to the mashed potatoes, I could eat a small piece of white bread. In time, I got stronger, and the day came when I ate, with relish, a whole bowlful of hearty meat and vegetable soup. What a day that was!

I was still too weak to walk to the fields where they were harvesting, so the brigadier assigned me to work in a field closer to home. I was supposed to pile up the sheaves but I was too weak and made little progress.

After I got stronger, I was sent, along with other workers, to a field about 10 kilometres away. Since we walked to the fields, it was too far, to go home at night. So we stayed there all week long. We started work very early in the morning before sunrise. Since the temperatures were unbearably hot from noon until 3 p.m., we were allowed to rest during that time. Then we worked again until dark. Twice a day we got something to eat and water to drink. But we couldn't wash, not even our faces. The water in the barrels was for us and the horses to drink. The dust of the fields stuck to our sweaty bodies and faces and soon we were filthy. After sleeping in the fields all night, I smoothed out my crumpled dress the best I could, and, not having a comb, opened my braids and ran my fingers through my long brown hair, then braided it again. Each time, clumps of hair came out. Eventually, I lost all my hair and I covered my bald head with a kerchief. At last, when we did return to our village, we headed straight for the Dnieper, girls to one bay and boys to another. We undressed and dove into the cool water and scrubbed our bodies clean. Meanwhile, our clothes, which we washed in the river, lay on the rocks to dry. What a relief to be clean again!

One day, the girls in my brigade were assigned to unload 100-pound sacks of wheat at a train station. I grabbed one end of a sack, another girl grabbed the other end, and straining every muscle, we heaved the sack into a freight car. We worked like this all day, our arms and fingers screaming in pain, while a man sat on a wagon and watched us. His work assignment was to drive the wagon, so I'm sure he felt justified in not helping us. The next day, when I was assigned to work in the dusty fields, I considered myself lucky.

One day, our work assignment was to carry boards to the builders of a dam near Einlage (between Burwalde and Chortitza.) I was intrigued by the interesting contraption across the Dnieper, built by foreign engineers, which would bring electricity into our villages. I could hardly fathom the wonder of having light at the flick of a switch. At this work site, each of us workers received a can of pork and beans. I'll never forget the delicious taste! I wished I could stay and work there forever, but the next day I was moved again.

That was the last year I was at home. In the fall of 1934, I left home for the first time to go to my aunt Lentje's place in Neuendorf. My aunt, a reputable seamstress, was usually paid in food. Having more than enough for her family, she offered to take care of one of my mother's children. My sister, Tina, stayed with her for one summer, and when she had to go back to school, I took her place. That was a great help for my mother, what with my father gone, and the family starving.

CHAPTER FOUR

My Marriage to Isaac Loewen

B ECAUSE FOOD WAS still scarce at home, in the summer of 1934, my sister Tina went to live with Tante Lentje in Neuendorf. My emaciated fourteen-year-old sister needed more nourishment. In the fall, when Tina returned to school in Nieder-Chortitza, I exchanged places with her so that my portion of food could be used to feed the others at home. My aunt found me a job as a nanny at the home of Cornelius and Anna Peters. In return for looking after their four children and helping with the chores, I received room and board. As soviet leader of Neuendorf, Cornelius earned enough food for his family of six *and* a border.

My cousin Neta, two years younger than I, invited me to come with her to her youth group, but I was ashamed to go. My hair still hadn't grown much and I always wore a kerchief. Mr. Peters used to tease me about it. "Do you have ears under that kerchief?" he'd ask with a twinkle in his eyes. In a few months my hair grew back in, soft and fine, like baby's hair, and curly! Since the fashion of the day was long, straight hair fixed in a bun at the nape of the neck, I waited a few more weeks until my hair grew long enough so I could pull it back tightly and tie a ribbon around it. But I was pleased with the soft brown curls that framed my angular face. For the first time in my life, I could almost believe that I was somewhat pretty. I accepted my cousin's invitation to youth group and began attending regularly.

I also attended the Mennonite church at the far end of Neuendorf. The communists had already closed most of the churches in Chortitza but Neuendorf's church, served by Pastor Giesbrecht, was still open. On Sunday after church, I walked down tree shaded streets through the village to my room at the Peters. Some days, I heard foot steps behind me. I guessed Isaac Loewen, a neighbour about my age, was also on his way home, but it never occurred to me to slow down to let him catch up with me. I was painfully shy and he intimidated me. He was 6'4", blond, and very handsome. Besides, he had an important job as a machinist at the kholkoz and received much better pay than other boys his age.

One of my chores was to haul water from a well which happened to be on the yard of Isaac's home. His mother, Helena Loewen, had lost her husband in an industrial accident some years ago, leaving her with five children to raise. Occasionally I would see her—a large woman with a stern look who never smiled or greeted me. People said that she was the kind of woman you didn't want to have as an enemy. Sometimes, I would see Isaac in the yard with one of his brothers, but I pretended not to notice. I would let the bucket down the well, then quickly haul it up. In my hurry to get away, I would slosh water over my feet. Sometimes Isaac and his brother seemed to be talking extra loudly as though they wanted my attention, but I didn't look up. I felt quite certain no boy would ever love me. I was too shy and plain.

One Saturday in the late afternoon, Isaac called at the Peters' house. *He's come to discuss business,* I thought, and hurried into the garden. Isaac worked as a machinist on a tractor brigade and, no doubt, had come to report to the soviet leader. I stayed in the garden and kept myself busy hoeing. Half an hour later, Isaac left the house and passed me in the garden. I kept my eyes on the ground, but once he entered the street, I stared at his back. It seemed to me that he walked with a swagger.

The next weekend when Isaac called, I left the house again so he could visit with the Peters. After his brief visit, Anna Peters called me aside. "Why do you leave when Isaac comes?" she teased. "You don't think he wants to visit us, do you?"

I stared at her in bewilderment.

"Come now," Anna's eyes twinkled merrily. "He's never been that interested in his neighbours before."

My heart raced. Could he really be interested in *me*?

"But, he's never even talked to me," I stammered.

"He doesn't have a chance," she laughed. "You always run away."

From then on, I spent extra time on my hair, and I lingered a little longer at the well, but I did not see much of Isaac that summer. His tractor brigade often took him to fields far from home, which meant he was gone for several weeks at a time with only an occasional weekend at home.

One summer evening, I saw Isaac all dressed up riding a shiny, new bicycle past the garden where I was hoeing. He rode by several times and it dawned on me that he was trying to catch my attention, which, of course, he had. A bicycle was a novelty in our village. As he entered the Peters' yard, he speeded up. Suddenly I heard a thud. Out of the corner of my eye, I saw a cloud of ashes billowing out of the ash heap near the summer kitchen. A tall, grey figure emerged, jumped onto the bicycle, and without a backward glance, pedalled away at high speed. About an hour later, Isaac rode by again but he had changed his clothes. I chuckled realizing how hard he was trying to capture my attention.

One day as Isaac visited the Peters' house he stopped in the garden and handed me a letter saying, "I met somebody from your village, and he gave me this letter for you." I didn't recognize the sender's name, so I handed it back to him. "The letter is for someone else," I said. "I don't know this man." Later, I discovered Isaac had written the letter himself to see how I would react.

Another Sunday, as I was walking home from church, I heard Isaac's foot steps speeding up. Feeling anxious and shy, I speeded up also. But Isaac caught up with me. "Why are you trying to run away from me?" he asked in a teasing manner. "I don't bite, you know." I laughed. Soon we were chatting together amiably. At the Peters' gate, as I prepared to go inside, Isaac asked me, "Do you have a special friend at home?" I looked into his earnest grey eyes, set deep in a handsome face, his dark blond hair combed back from a high forehead, and shook my head no. "Then may I call on you sometimes?" he asked.

"Yes," I smiled.

Now that the ice was broken, we always walked home from church together. He came to see me at the Peters whenever he was home. We dated a whole summer and through the next winter, and our romance blossomed. When the Peters were home we would go for long walks. On winter evenings, we would visit in the Peters' house. They always found a reason to leave the house so we could be alone. Isaac was an intelligent man with a good sense of humour and I enjoyed his company very much. But sometimes he would be so tired from working long hours at the kolkhoz that he fell asleep. I would continue knitting or darning without waking him—just having him near me was pleasure enough. When it was time for him to go home, I would gently wake him up; he would mumble an apology, and promise to be back soon. (By the way, I never did tell him I knew about the ash heap incident. *No need to embarrass him,* I thought.)

One evening, Isaac told me his mother planned to marry D. Sawatsky, a widower, who had five young children, the youngest just three years old. After the wedding, Isaac's mother would be going to live in the Sawatsky's beautiful brick house, taking brothers Peter and Hans and sister Lena with her. "It's not going to be a happy family," Isaac said. His mother was far too independent and she was quarrelsome by nature.

Suddenly Isaac's grey eyes became soft and shiny. "Neta, I don't want to move with Mother, but I don't want to live alone either," he said. "Will you marry me?"

"Yes," I whispered. "Yes, I will."

"Then we're engaged now." He leaned forward and kissed me for the first time.

Isaac was twenty-one years old and I was twenty-three.

Soon we made a trip to Nieder-Chortitza to announce our engagement and to invite my family and friends to our wedding scheduled on Sunday, June 2, 1935. It was the last day the communists allowed public services to be held in the Neuendorf Mennonite Church. In the morning, a baptismal service would take place, and in the afternoon, Pastor Giesbrecht would marry us.

The day was hot and sultry. I borrowed my cousin's white dress. Then I fussed with my hair. It was longer and straighter now and I could twist it into a small bun at the nape of my neck.

"You're a beautiful bride," Anna Peters smiled. "And you'll make Isaac a good wife."

I blushed.

Nervously, I waited by the door for my bridegroom to call on me. As was the custom, Isaac and I would be walking to the church together. Cornelius and Anna, all ready to go, came into the kitchen. "Where's Isaac?"

"He hasn't come yet."

"Better go get him then."

Yes, it was late. What could be keeping him?

Feeling rather conspicuous in my wedding gown, I walked across the street, past the well, and across the big yard to the Loewen residence. I met Isaac at the door, dressed in his father's black suit, white shirt, and black leather shoes. "We'll have to wait for my mother," he whispered.

His mother, a big woman, seemed unusually agitated this morning. Suddenly, she stopped in front of us, looked down at Isaac's feet, and cried, "Ike, you rascal, you're using my shoe laces."

"Mine are knotted," he said, "so I took yours."

"What am I going to use?"

"It's my wedding day." Isaac shrugged. "I can't have knotted shoe laces."

Hurriedly, his mother ripped up a rag and blackened the thin strips on the back of a frying pan, then she laced her shoes with them. We were ready to go.

As Isaac and I walked to the church and breathed deeply the fragrance of acacia blossoms, we were hardly aware of his mother's grumbling behind us. From every homestead, people poured into the road and headed for the church. Soon the church was packed with an overflow crowd standing at the door and spilling into the courtyard.

It was a memorable day. A mass choir filled the church with rousing hymns. Several stirring sermons followed.

Many young people, from our own village as well as other villages, were baptized. Finally, the time came for our wedding. My two girlfriends walked ahead of us, carrying wedding chairs decorated in flowers and vines, and placed them in front of the altar. Isaac and I followed, walking down the aisle together, then sat down on the chairs in front of Pastor Giesbrecht. I'm afraid I don't remember much about our wedding ceremony; I can't even remember the special Scripture he gave us for our life together. I was too nervous and excited. At the end of the day everyone shared in the Lord's Supper, and Isaac and I, as newlyweds, participated.

Anna Peters had prepared a lovely meal for our reception, but since her food supply was so meagre, she invited only some of my immediate family: my mother, my sisters Tina and Annie, and my brother, Gerhard. My brothers, Henry and Peter, were billeted in another home. But by the time they arrived, the family had eaten and the food was all gone. I didn't find out until much later that my brothers had gone home hungry. I felt badly about it, but I couldn't have done anything about it anyway: there simply wasn't enough food to go around.

A funny thing happened to my family as they walked thirty kilometres from Nieder-Chortitza to Neuendorf to attend our wedding. To save their shoes, they walked barefoot, their shoes slung over their shoulders. They were hot and dusty and weary.

Some distance out of Neuendorf, a bus stopped and the driver invited them to get inside. Gratefully, they accepted the ride. Later, as they were leaving, the driver demanded money. My mother looked at him in astonishment.

"We don't have any."

"You don't expect to travel for free?

"Yes—I mean—no," my mother stammered. No contract had been made and she had assumed he was doing them a favour.

"Then I'll take these." He snatched Tina's shoes off her shoulder.

"I can't go to the wedding without my shoes," Tina cried.

Every passenger on the bus was now watching this interesting drama. One man shouted, "Ladies, where are you going?"

"To Isaac Loewen's wedding."

"I know him," the man said. "I'll pay for their fares." It turned out he was a friend of the Loewen family.

The bus driver took the money, returned the shoes to Tina, and then drove away.

Of course, my husband reimbursed the kind passenger who paid for the ride. But this incident became a friendly joke around our village, "Poor Isaac, your new family is already costing you money," people said.

After the wedding, as we sat and chatted in Anna Peter's lovely living room, Isaac and I in our wedding attire, a thunderstorm raged outside. Rain pelted on the window panes. We waited until it stopped, then Isaac announced it was time to go home. He reached for my hand but I pulled it away. "I can't go with you tonight," I said. "Suzie (the Peter's daughter) is ill and I must stay with her," I explained. So my newly-wed husband went to his bed alone. It took me four days before I had the courage to accompany him to his house for night and only after he'd promised I could sleep in the guest room until I felt comfortable sleeping with him. I was that shy! Soon after our wedding, Isaac returned to work on a distant kolkhoz. Then my new husband came home only on weekends.

Soon after our wedding day, a notice was nailed to the church door forbidding any religious meetings in the future. Men carried the pews and altar outside and loaded them into trucks. The Neuendorf Mennonite Church became a soviet granary.

Two weeks later, Isaac's mother and D. Sawatsky were married in a civil ceremony in his home. Mother moved out of the Loewen homestead, and Isaac and I moved in. Times were hard our first year of marriage. There was so little food to buy. The stores were practically empty. When a shipment of sugar, flour, or salt came in, I would rise very early and hurry to the store to join the bread lines. People rubbed their hands and stomped their feet in the cold early morning air. There was a sense of camaraderie among us until the doors opened. Then, all civilities aside, the mob pushed forward. "Leave some for us," people further back called to those in front. Some times, after waiting for hours, the groceries were all gone by the time my turn came. Many people, like me, went home empty-handed. But I was luckier than most, for Isaac was able to get some food on the black market. Besides driving a tractor, Isaac was also the chief repairman of combines and tractors for his brigade. He worked long days and evenings from early spring to late autumn. For this reason, he received more grain than ordinary workers did which he then traded at the black market for eggs, meat and flour.

I also planted a large vegetable garden, and soon we had tomatoes, cabbages, beans, potatoes and beets. When the fruit in the orchard ripened, I dried apricots, pears, and plums; I also pickled and canned vegetables for our winter use. And in this way we managed to get enough food to eat.

Stalin's Great Purge of Russia

The mid 1930s marked the height of Stalin's great purge of Russia when millions were shot, imprisoned, or banished to Siberia. Towards evening, when a blue car entered our village, terror filled our hearts: Stalin's secret police were stalking the streets. Before morning several good, strong, young men would be gone, arrested and deported. Most were never heard from again. No explanations or trials were given. These men had done nothing wrong. They were good men who had served their country well. One morning, a very distraught Anna told me that the KGB had taken Cornelius away. *Cornelius?* I was shocked. He was the soviet leader of our village, after all. Anna's story was so typical of other households which suffered a similar fate that I will tell it here.

"Late at night, there was a heavy pounding on the door and a man shouted, 'Open this door,'" Anna said. "Cornelius whispered to me, 'Be brave, Anna.' Then he walked to the door and opened it. Two KGB rushed in. The children, shocked by the sudden intrusion, began to cry.

"Grab your stuff and come with us," a man barked in Russian.

"Where are you taking my husband?" I asked.

"You'll find out in the morning."

"Cornelius picked up each of the children and hugged them goodbye. Then he embraced me and whispered, 'Don't give up hope, dear. Pray that our heavenly Father will bring us back together soon'." But as Anna was telling me, she was sobbing bitterly. "I don't know if I'll ever see Cornelius again," she said.

Each morning after a visitation by the KGB, the news travelled from door to door which men had been taken. In rapid whispers, we heard the names of the unfortunate captives. One morning, Hans Wiebe, my cousin Lena's husband, was gone. They were newlyweds like us. I shuddered: *When will it be Isaac's turn?*

Although Anna Peters and the other bereaved women sought an explanation at the communist office, either no reason was given, or their men were accused of being German spies.

Anti-German sentiment was strong since World War I when German soldiers had marched into Russia. Still, Mennonites were law-abiding, tax-paying citizens, who did not believe in war. Throughout more than 150 years in Russia, their ancestors had worked hard to serve their adopted country. They had coaxed out of the wild Ukrainian steppes fertile orchards and prosperous farms. They had built hospitals, schools and factories. Some had worked in the forests of Russia. Clearly, Mennonites loved their adopted country.

Stalin's purge began with the Russian army. One day I received the sad news that my brother Henry, a soldier in the Red Army, was taken. He and another friend from Nieder-Chortitza were accused of treason. The men were interrogated and asked to sign a confession. Even though Henry was tortured, he refused to sign. His friend signed and was executed the next morning. Henry was sentenced to hard labour for life, and sent to Siberia to work in the coal mines. We would not see him again until many years later. Next Stalin targeted minority groups such as Jewish people and other ethnic people, like the Mennonites. Still, in the tide of Stalin's ruthless purge, many innocent Russian men and families were also sent to Siberia. Stalin showed no mercy.

On evenings when the blue car entered Neuendorf, I found it impossible to go to sleep. I followed Isaac around not wanting to let him out of my sight. Wide awake in bed,

I listened for the drone of a motor, the barking of dogs, and the stomping of boots on gravel that would announce the arrival of the dreaded KGB.

"Neta, go to sleep," Isaac tried to soothe my fears. "The communists aren't going to take me. They need me to fix the combines and tractors here at home." He stroked my hair with his large hand. "How else can they bring in the harvest?" His reassuring logic made sense, but I still worried. Just in case, I packed a small suitcase which sat near the door. If the KGB came for him, at least he'd have a few essentials to take with him.

Stalin's determination to purge Russia of Christianity increased. It now became a criminal offence to own a Bible, to say table grace, or to sing hymns. Children were quizzed at school about their family practices. "Do your parents say prayers before a meal or at bedtime? Do they tell you Bible stories?" the teacher asked. If so, it was reason enough to banish them. Parents were terrified; the state was turning their children into government spies. Still, most parents remained strong in their faith.

This reminds me of an incident which happened the Christmas before we were married. A group of us girls were in the Soviet Club House supposedly sewing, but we had no material to work with, so, to pass the time, we drew dress patterns on paper. On Christmas Day, we began to reminisce about some of the celebrations and programs we had enjoyed as children. Quietly, Lena began to hum a Christmas carol and Lisa chimed in. Soon more tremulous voices joined the swelling chorus.

The next day, a very angry komsomol demanded who had started the singing. Nobody answered. "All right then, I'll punish all of you," he stormed.

"I started it," Lena jumped to her feet. "Lisa and me."

"A criminal offence," the man glowered. "I could have you and your parents sent to Siberia."

He called for Lisa to stand up and come forward. She fell to her knees before the man and begged for mercy. Lena, on the other hand, stood tall. With a raised fist she yelled, "I'm twenty-one years old. If you think singing a few Christmas carols is a crime, then punish me, but leave my parents alone."

Lena became my heroine that day. *I hope I'll be as brave when my time comes*, I thought.

A year later, the overseer himself was banished to Siberia. Stalin's tyranny spared no one.

"I'm A Married Man Now!"

Several months after Isaac and I were married, Isaac's mother surprised me with a visit. One morning, as I was doing laundry in the summer kitchen, a wagon filled with furniture and personal belongings, clattered onto our yard. Mother Loewen hopped down and called to her children, "Get down now. We're home again."

Has she come to stay? I didn't have to wonder long, for she called to me, "Neta help me move this stuff into the house." I dried my hands on my apron and followed her into the house. In the bedroom she ordered me to empty out the dresser drawers. I scooped up Isaac's and my belongings, then I watched as Helena filled the drawers with her own and her children's clothing.

When Isaac returned home from work, he was shocked to see our personal stuff pushed into a corner of the kitchen while his mother presided over the home as though she had never left.

"You've come to stay?" Isaac's eyebrows shot up.

"Of course. I'm not going to be nursemaid to Sawatsky's kids."

"You were warned," Isaac said.

"Never mind, " she said and smiled smugly. "I'm back home where I belong."

"But Neta and I—"

Mother waved a large hand. "I've thought of everything," she said dismissively. "We'll build a room in the barn. You and Neta can live there."

"Mother!" my husband's voice was tense. "The barn is no place for my family."

"You will do as you're told," his mother said.

Isaac jumped to his feet and banged his fist on the table. "I'm a married man now," he shouted.

"Please, Isaac," I said, trying to make peace. "It will work out." But neither mother nor son were willing to negotiate. That evening, Isaac and I gathered up our belongings and moved to Cornelius Neudorf's house where we rented a room. But on that first night, we slept on the floor in their summer porch.

As a tractor machinist, Isaac earned more wheat than we needed for ourselves. Soon we sold some wheat at the market, and with the money, we bought a bed, table and chairs, a sofa, a cow and a piglet. It was a good beginning for our own home.

Lena, Our First Child

Food was still very scarce. To help Isaac's mother out, I encouraged his brothers and sister to eat supper with us. "Tell Mother she's welcome," I said, but she never came. Sometimes I sent fresh buns and soup with them, but my gifts were not acknowledged. Helena made it very obvious that she was angry with me. When she saw me walking towards her on the street, she quickly crossed over to the other side and pretended not to see me. She spread malicious gossip about me: "Until *she* came along my son and I got along just fine," she told our neighbours. "But this no-good wife of his has turned my son against me." She'd give a little sniffle to show how deeply she was suffering under her son's apparent rejections. Isaac told me not to let his mother's ornery behaviour bother me. "Mother's always been a cantankerous woman," he said. But I yearned for peace in the family and I was deeply grieved that there should be a division.

Meanwhile Isaac was very busy working as machinist for the kolkhoz. He was responsible to fix all the tractors and combines for his brigade. He was also the town's electrician. When the power lines were down in Neuendorf, he was the one called to fix the problem.

One day Isaac brought home some planks of hardwood. I wondered where he had managed to find them, for wood was scarce in our area. He merely smiled. "The baby will need a cradle," he said. After supper, he went to his work bench, carefully measuring and cutting, sanding, varnishing, and glueing the pieces together. *Isaac can do anything he puts his mind to*, I realized. The cradle, a beautiful work of art, was ready when our first child was born on July 11, 1936. We named her Helena after Isaac's mother, Lena for short. "Your mother will be pleased," I told Isaac. "Perhaps now we can be friends."

"Don't count on it," he said.

As my eyes rested on the sleeping child, my heart almost burst with maternal pride. *Was any child more beautiful?* Our daughter resembled her blond, blue-eyed father. *Good thing, for I am no beauty*, I thought. I picked up a small fist and playfully extended each little finger. *How pleased her grandmother will be that her first grandchild resembles her side of the family!*

Every day, I waited for Isaac's mother to pay us a visit, but several months went by, and she didn't come. One day as I finished nursing the baby and put her back in her cradle, I had a brilliant idea. Helena's birthday was tomorrow. *I will surprise her,* I thought, *I'll bring Lena to her."*

When I neared her house, I heard voices. *A birthday party! Maybe I shouldn't have come.* But my arms ached and my heart ached even more. Timidly, I knocked on the door. Mother yelled, "Come in."

I opened the door, then I hesitated. The room was filled with women and, now, all eyes were fixed on me. One woman jumped to her feet and said, "Show us your baby, Neta." I stepped forward and opened the blanket. Soon other women crowded round and remarked on my beautiful baby. But Isaac's mother pretended not to notice; she was very busy fixing something at the back of the room. One woman yelled, "Helena, come on. Come, see your grandchild."

She came and glanced down at the baby.

"Not a bit like Isaac," she exclaimed. "He was never that ugly."

"Helena, how can you say that?" one woman remonstrated. "They've named her after you."

"They could have named her after an old cow, for all I care."

I turned abruptly and left the house. Tears blurred the garden path as I stumbled along it. I was nearly at the road when Helena shouted, "Hey, come back. You can't be that sensitive."

I did not go back.

When I told Isaac, he was furious.

In the next three months, Lena grew rolls of baby fat. Her peach fuzz gave way to fine, blond hair. She smiled easily and her bright eyes followed me around.

One day in late October, while Isaac and I were eating our supper, a shadow darkened the window. Could it be his mother? My pulse quickened. A sharp rap on the door, and Helena's ample frame stood in the doorway. Without as much as a greeting, she came into the kitchen.

Isaac's face registered surprise but he maintained his composure. I got a chair for her to sit down.

His mother lifted Lena out of her crib, then sat down with her on her lap. "Everybody tells me what a gorgeous baby my first grandchild is," she crooned. "I had to come and see for myself."

She opened a bag and pulled out some of Isaac's baby clothes: a crocheted hat and a little jacket with a crochet collar. But nothing fit; it was all too small.

At first, Isaac's mother talked amiably as though there had never been a misunderstanding between us, then her tone became more business-like. "I've heard you've done well at work," she said to her son. "You must have more wheat than you need."

"Yes, I've done well," my husband answered, a glint of amusement in his grey eyes. He knew all too well what his mother was driving at.

"Can you give me some wheat?" she asked matter-of-fact. "I could trade it at the market."

Isaac gave her what she asked for.

From then on, we were welcome at the Loewen homestead and his mother also visited us.

But often mother and son argued and I much preferred visiting his other relatives.

Lena was an inquisitive child. Once she started to walk, she explored every inch of her surroundings. I would find her in the kolkhoz stable toddling among the horses, her chubby body brushing up against their strong legs. She offered the horses fistfuls of hay and giggled when their lips curled around her chubby hand. She followed the chickens and the rooster around the yard and splashed in their drinking water. She chased the cat, and one day, I found her playing with a dead mouse. "Dirty!" I shouted. "Leave that thing alone." Her blue eyes filled with tears as I tossed it into the garbage. My daughter seemed to have an affinity for animals, even dead ones.

I could never be sure what my toddler would do next. One day as I came in from the barn, I saw her sitting on the kitchen table beneath a window. Wielding a pair of sharp scissors, she was snipping her own design into the fabric of the curtains. "Lena, no!" I shouted and took the scissors out of her hand. Another day, we were going to visit my family in Nieder-Chortitza. I had dressed Lena in her starched little Sunday dress, red hat, and shoes. While I was fixing my hair, she slipped out of the house. When Isaac went to look for her, he found her splashing in the chicken's water. Of course, her little dress was ruined. "This child needs stern discipline," Isaac said and gave her a spanking.

"Where is that child now?" I fumed. A few moments ago, my three-year-old had been playing quietly on the floor beside my chair. *I must have dozed off while nursing the baby.* "Lena," I called as I checked every room. No response. I placed the baby back into her cradle and began to search for my toddler in the yard and the garden. No Lena. I asked the neighbours on either side of the street if they had seen her. They shook their heads no but they agreed to look for her in their own yards and gardens. Meanwhile, the sun was dipping behind the tops of acacia trees lining the street. Soon it would be dark. The one place I hadn't searched yet was Helena's yard. Fearing a lecture from her, I had hesitated to involve her. Now I hurried over. As I scanned my mother-in-law's garden, my heart skipped a beat. Beside the pole beans, I spied something red bobbing up and down between the rows. I shielded my eyes against the slanting rays of the setting sun, and looked closer. A little girl with a red hat askew on a tousled blond head, was sitting among a pile of tomatoes she had yanked off the vines. Some tomatoes she'd squished between her chubby fingers and eaten, her sticky cheeks bearing evidence. Her dress was stained with tomato juice and speckled with seeds and bits of squished fruit. Her face and hands were yellow.

I pulled her up. "Naughty girl! Look what you've done now."

Taking her sticky little hand in mine, we walked towards Helena's house. My pulse raced as I knocked on my mother-in-law's door. She would be mad and rightly so.

Soon Helena came to the door. She looked at my flushed face, then down at her grandchild.

"I'm sorry, Mother," I stammered. "I found Lena in your garden. I'm afraid she's pulled off some of your tomatoes." I looked down at the ground. Then I quickly added, "I'll bring you some of mine when they ripen."

Helena looked at the child—her hair was standing up in spikes; her round cheeks were speckled with seeds; her dress was stiff like yellow cardboard. The older woman's mouth twitched a little, then she burst out laughing. "Don't worry," she said. "I'm sure she didn't get them all."

Like her grandmother, Anna Neudorf, our landlady, adored Lena and found her mischievous ways more amusing than her parents did. And like most older women do, she proceeded to spoil her by offering her treats. On those days, come supper time, Lena's stomach was full and she couldn't eat everything on her plate–a stern rule in our household. Her father, having finished his supper, would push back his chair from the table and reach for the leather strap. Placing Lena across his knee he gave her a loud slap. "Don't feed Lena anymore," I begged Anna, but she often did anyway. And so our little girl received many spankings. Her sobbing would tug at my heart and I'd bend down to pick her up, but her father would say, "Leave her. She's been disciplined." It sounds harsh now, but that was the German way.

Despite these painful episodes, Lena loved her father. When she heard the distant hum of his motorcycle nearing our home, she ran to get me. "Papa, balala," she said, pulling on my skirt. Lena wasn't the only one who heralded Isaac's noisy arrival. His was the only motorcycle in the village of Neuendorf and, therefore, quite a novelty. Children would come running to the road to wave. Young men, likewise, loved the loud noise; older men shook their heads at the formidable speed. It always thrilled me to see Isaac, astride on his bike, so handsome in his riding gear, come swinging into our yard.

Isaac had been promoted to brigadier, the boss of the tractor brigade, which meant he was supervising crews in far-away places. He bought the motorcycle so he could cover the long distances between the groups. Having transportation also meant that he could come home after work. I was thrilled to see more of my husband, also gratified that the bike brought him so much pleasure. In the winter, it provided transportation to the technical school in Zaporozhye where he studied mechanical engineering. Frequently he brought his little daughter a treat he had bought in the city: a toy or some sweets. Lena cherished the teddy bear her father gave her and lugged it around wherever she went. One time it was caught in the sprockets of the motorcycle parked in the summer porch. "Mitzi fast balala," she cried. Her father came over, loosed the teddy, and, handing it to her, patted her little head affectionately.

The first day Isaac brought the motorcycle home, his mother asked him for a ride. "Wait until I've made a proper back seat," Isaac remonstrated, but his mother was adamant–she wanted to be the first one to ride it. "Then climb on, and hold tight," her son said. The two took off in a roar. But before long, Isaac hit a bump in the road and his mother fell off. He wasn't aware of it at first and continued down the road. When he realized that she was no longer holding onto him, he turned around and went looking for her. He found her sitting on the road crying, perhaps not so much from bodily harm, as from having been humiliated in front of her neighbours. It became a joke in the village: Isaac lost his mother and he didn't even know it!

Isaac was very pleased with his motorcycle and he wanted me to share in his joy. He made a special seat for me and had a tailor sew a riding outfit for me. The suit was like a skirt, but it buttoned up front and back forming pant legs. The children would look at me and giggle, "Oh, a lady in pants!" They had never seen such a strange sight before. Isaac was a little too modern for me, I concluded, and one day, I took the buttons off and closed the button holes. Then I sewed up the panels making a proper skirt out of it. When he came home, I showed him my handiwork. He was disappointed and said I'd ruined a perfectly good riding outfit.

One day Isaac took me to a meadow outside the village for a lesson on how to ride solo on a motorcycle. "You know how to ride a bicycle," he said. "This isn't much different." I made a few successful rounds on the meadow. "Good," he said. "You've got the gist of it. Now you can drive home." I wasn't so sure I wanted to ride the motorcycle by myself into the village. But Isaac insisted, jumped onto his bicycle, and took off for home. So what could I do but get on that motorcycle? I revved up the motor and started down the road. Along came a herd of calves and I was heading straight for them. I swerved sharply to the right just missing a calf. But my front wheel hit a pothole and the bike jumped dangerously. I hung on for dear life and managed to stay on. Afraid of what else I might meet on the road, I stuck to the edge and bumped along from pothole to pothole. When I got to our gate, I meant to slow down to turn the corner, but I grabbed the wrong lever giving the bike *more* gas instead of less. The bike leaped forward and missed the driveway altogether. I crashed through the picket fence and came to rest in a heap near our front door. Of course, Isaac was standing there laughing. I picked myself up and announced, "That's the last time I'm ever driving this thing!"

Isaac also taught me to clean the motorcycle. He wanted me to learn how to take it apart and put it back together again, so he showed me all the mechanics. People began to tease me, calling me "the mechanic." But I was happy to do that as long as he didn't make me drive it.

Now that we had a motorcycle, we made frequent visits to my family in Nieder-Chortitza. My sister Annie spent many hours playing with Lena on the yard making sand castles or looking for sea shells beside the Dnieper. Our visit's always ended in *vaspa* (a small evening meal) together. My mother enjoyed watching Lena drink coffee from a shallow saucer. "That child's got a good constitution,"she laughed. "Shows character the way she drinks her prips." (Prips was made from roasted kernels of grain, not real coffee beans.)

Agnes, Our Second Child

Our second baby was born on April 26, 1938. We named her Agnes. She was a contented baby who slept hours on end. Lena loved her baby sister and spent much time by her cradle. Isaac was gone all week working and seeding the fields, and I was extremely busy with family chores. So I was glad for my oldest child's watchful eye on the baby. But Lena, just three-years-old, was too young for such a responsibility. Once, I heard Agnes' loud cry mixed in with Lena's screaming. I bolted into the house and saw the cradle tipped over with baby on the floor. Another time when I entered the house, I heard a funny, chortling noise coming from the cradle. I sprinted over to check on the baby. Agnes' little arms flailed the air, her tiny face was contorted and turning blue. She was choking! Hurriedly, I grabbed her, turned her upside down on my knee, and thumped her back. A small piece of bread popped from the baby's mouth. Soon the baby breathed normally and her face became a healthy pink. Beside the crib stood Lena with a piece of bread in her chubby hands. She had tried to feed the baby.

Now that we were a family of four, we had outgrown the small accommodation at the Neudorf's house and we moved to a two-room apartment in the Nick Kröker's house where I shared the kitchen, pantry, and cellar with our landlady. Tante Lentje (the seamstress) and cousins Neta and Lena were now our neighbours. Often I went to visit them and my aunt taught me how to sew. As I stitched garments for my babies, a dress for myself, and a shirt for Isaac, I remembered my father's words to me that day when I had to quit school in order to help with chores at home: "Don't cry, Neta, one day you will become a successful seamstress like Tante Lentje."

Isaac also bought me a sheep and a spinning wheel. His mother taught me how to spin the wool into yarn and I spent many happy hours at the spinning wheel and knitting sweaters for us all.

To fuel the kitchen stove, we used straw and dried maize cobs. One day the straw was wet and it wouldn't burn. Acrid smoke drifted through the kitchen. At this rate, supper would not be ready when Isaac came home. Wanting to hurry up the cooking process, I took some black, greasy, liquid Isaac had left in a jar after changing the oil in his motorcycle and dumped it onto the smouldering fire. A cloud of smoke rose. Going closer, I blew upon the smouldering heap. An explosion roared and the force of it slammed my body against the wall across the kitchen. Lena screamed and dropped to her knees beside me. Pulling on my sleeves she kept saying, "Up, Mommy. Up, Mommy."

My face puffed up leaving narrow slits for my eyes. Blisters developed into ugly sores.

When Mrs. Kröker came home, she hurried into her living room, plucked a succulent aloe vera leaf off a large plant in a pot, slit it open with a paring knife, and held it towards me. "Dab your face with this," she said. "Twice a day." That dear lady brought me a new leaf every morning decimating her aloe vera plant.

For many days Lena would sit beside me when I fed the fire. "Come away, Mommy," she'd coax pulling on my sleeve. Or she would touch my face saying softly, "Owie?" Little by little my face healed up, leaving no scar.

But my accident was minor compared to my second daughter's accident. One supper time, Mrs.Kröker had placed a bowl of boiling soup on the kitchen table. Agnes, just three years old, stood on her tip toes to take a closer look at the tantalizing food. But Rita, the Kröker's daughter, pushed her away, saying, "You can't look." Trying to break her fall, Agnes grabbed the table cloth. The soup tureen teetered, then fell, dumping the boiling soup over her.

Hearing her screams, I bolted into the room. Agnes cowered beside the kitchen table, bits of potatoes and cabbage clinging to her dress. I stripped off her dress as quickly as I could and to my horror, I saw patches of her skin stuck to my hands.

For three days Agnes hovered between life and death. Once more I used aloe vera juice but there wasn't enough to cover her body. Many days I sat outside holding her on my lap with just a sheet covering her. Lena sat beside me holding her teddy bear on her lap. "Baby, owie?" she kept asking. Thank God, Agnes also recovered and today she carries no scars.

Fred, Our Son; Dysentery and War

On September 25, 1940 a son was born to us. We named him Isaac after his father, but later his name was changed to Fred, so for convenience I shall call him Fred throughout. Since Neuendorf had no doctor or hospital, our son was delivered by a midwife in a maternity house. After the birth, I stayed in bed for one week as was the custom in those days. Isaac hurried home from Zaporozhye to see his newborn son. As he gazed down at his sleeping child, his face glowed with joy and pride. To have a son of his own, was a special honour in our Mennonite culture.

When Fred was a chubby eight-month-old, there was an outbreak of dysentery in our village and some children died. Soon my baby also developed the dreaded symptoms of fever, diarrhea and vomiting. He lost weight and became listless. Being worried, Isaac took Fred and me to the Children's Hospital in Zaporozhye, across the Dnieper.

As we checked in our baby, I marvelled at the ease with which my husband spoke the Ukrainian language with the doctor and nurses. I could understand only a little and speak even less. The nurse took Fred out of my arms and carried him away. Since I was still breastfeeding him, I stayed at the hospital. As I said goodbye to Isaac, I wondered how I would manage in this Ukrainian city on my own.

A woman showed me my accommodation—a large room with many beds—and pointed to one bed. Mine, obviously. Then she handed me a breast pump and a small bottle so I could express my milk and bring it to the hospital each day for my baby's feeding. She also gave me a blue gown which I was to wear whenever I entered the hospital.

Fifteen other women shared the room with me. They were all Russian and I could not communicate with them. When my roommates found out I was German, they became distant.

Only the woman whose bed was adjacent to mine was friendly to me.

Two days passed. Each morning I delivered my bottle of milk at the reception desk, hoping for a nurse to show me my baby, but nobody did, and nobody offered to tell me where he was. On my way back to the rooming house, I passed the morgue. Once I saw a man deliver a bundle the size of a small child. Fear shot through me. Was it Fred? I had no way of knowing because nobody told me anything. All night I tossed in my bed fearing the absolute worst: *My baby has died and they won't tell me.* As dawn streaked the eastern sky, I quickly dressed, and snuck out of the room. I hurried past the morgue, climbed the stairs to the main entrance of the hospital, and pushed through the heavy door. A woman tried to block me, but I shoved her away. "I want to see my baby," I choked.

I bolted up three flights of stairs to the third floor—I'd heard one woman say that's where her baby was—and entered a large open ward. Rows upon rows of cribs lined the walls. In some, babies were crying. I began to walk down the right side, peering into each crib looking for the familiar face of my child. No Fred. Then I walked slowly up the left side, peering into each little face. Still no Fred. "He has died," I sobbed, "just as I thought." My loud sobs attracted a nurse with a round, soft face.

"My baby," I choked. "Where's my baby?"

The nurse took my hand and led me to a small room with one bed in it. Fred's small body hardly made an indent in the large blanket covering him. His pinched little face framed huge, glassy eyes. I called him, but he didn't move. He stared right passed me as though he couldn't see me. His spindly arms lay listless on the covers. *Is he dead?* I stared at his little chest. *Thank God, he's still breathing.*

"Are you feeding him?" I asked with a surge of anger. (Suddenly I remembered my Russian.) "He needs a little milk every five minutes."

The nurse nodded. She must have felt sorry for me, for from that day on, I received a report every morning about my baby's condition.

In the afternoon of June 22, 1941, I went for a walk in the city. I was surprised to see so many army jeeps and soldiers in the streets. Something ominous was going on, but I didn't know what it could be. When I returned to my room, my roommates were talking in loud voices. They became even more agitated when they saw me. By their hostile stares, I sensed they were angry with me. Why the sudden hostility? I listened carefully. With my limited Russian, I figured it had to do with Germany being at war, so they would have a natural aversion to me, a German.

In the morning, a nurse came to our rooming house. "Every woman must come to work," she said. "Report at the hospital immediately."

I hurried to the designated area. All day we cut newspapers into strips, then using a mixture of flour and water, we pasted them diagonally across the windowpanes.

"Why are we doing this?" I asked.

"When the bombs fall the windows won't shatter."

"Bombs. Here?" I was incredulous.

"Germany has invaded our country."

Dear God, no! Fear jolted me. My body went numb, then I began to tremble. *What will become of us German-speaking Mennonites?* Now I understood the hostile glances I had received in the morning.

In the evening, the head nurse came again to urge the women to come to work at the hospital.

"We must prepare for an emergency," she said. But they stared sullenly at her as though that had nothing to do with them. Her face flushed. "Only one woman showed up for work today," she said angrily. "And she is a German."

She turned and stomped out of the room.

All the next day, I worked in the hospital basement. Again, none of the women from my ward showed up.

In the evening, Isaac came to see me. "Germany has invaded Russia," he said.

"I've already been told."

"It will be very bad for us Germans." Isaac looked worried.

"I want to go home," I said. "Fred is not getting the care he needs anyway."

"Wait a day," Isaac said. "Our village is in turmoil. The German army is advancing rapidly. *Blitzkrieg*, they call it. The Russians have ordered complete evacuation of every piece of machinery, every animal, every sack of grain... Our tractor brigade will soon be going east across the Dnieper."

"Please, take me home," I repeated. To be separated at a time like this was unthinkable.

"I'll come for you tomorrow."

As I watched Isaac's motorcycle disappear around the bend, I wanted to run after him.

I felt alone in a very hostile world.

The next afternoon, Isaac returned. We went to the ward and claimed our baby. They seemed relieved to be rid of us.

"Please give us a bottle of water for our baby," Isaac said to the nurse.

"No, he'll die anyway," she replied.

We stood rooted to the floor. "The journey is long. It's hot—"

"Just go," she said.

Isaac and I didn't argue. Anti-German sentiment would soon be part of every day for us.

The road was hot and dusty. In Chortitza, Isaac stopped the motor bike and walked to a house to ask for water. I unrolled the blanket and peeked at our baby. Was he still alive? Thank God, yes! His little chest was still moving. A few minutes later, when my husband brought a bottle of water, I opened my baby's parched mouth and poured in a few drops. He swallowed.

When I placed Fred into his familiar cradle, he opened his eyes wide. A little smile formed on his lips and my heart swelled. *He knows he's home,* I thought.

CHAPTER FIVE

Russia is at War with Germany

THE FOLLOWING DAY, Isaac and his whole tractor brigade drove their machines east across the Dnieper. It was a sad farewell. Women clung to their men as though they would never see them again. Besides the worry of my husband, I had the worry of my sick child. I had heard that in a neighbouring village lived a woman who had studied medicine. She might be able to help me. Isaac's mother agreed to look after the girls while I walked to Schönhorst carrying little Fred. By road it was only a few kilometres away. But the road was jammed with army trucks and tanks. I abandoned the road and walked across the fields. It was a big detour, but my son wasn't heavy. He was so thin.

Mrs. Dyck gave Fred a few drops of medicine. "He will sleep now," she said. "Keep his tummy nice and warm. In two days you must come again."

"Couldn't you give me the medicine so I can save myself a walk?"

She shook her head no. "The medicine is very strong. I will give it to him myself."

The medicine made the baby's mouth very dry and he found it difficult to swallow. So I chewed a little bread, mixing it with my saliva, then I popped it into his mouth. In this way, he was able to get some nourishment. After three visits, I noticed a slight improvement. Fred was gaining strength and he was becoming more alert and playful. If only Isaac could see him now. But where was his tractor brigade? Deep into Russia, no doubt. Would the men be allowed to return?

When I talked with the other wives, my fears were confirmed. "We'll never see our men again," they said. "The communists won't let them come home and deserters will be shot."

I was wild with worry. During Stalin's great purge, many men were ripped from their families, yet Isaac was spared. We had made it through the worst, I thought, and now in this unexpected way, my husband was snatched away from me and I hadn't even said a proper good-bye. Guilt plagued me that he went ill-prepared for the dangerous journey. I should have packed more clothes for him; I should have packed more food.

Late one night, I heard a knock on the door. Hurriedly I opened it.

"Isaac!" I screamed. "How did you get here?"

"Not so loud," he whispered. "I deserted—"

Isaac had realized the further he went into Russia, the less likely he would be able to return home. On the third night, he abandoned his tractor and fled on foot. During the day he hid in grain fields or in the woods; at night he crept towards the west. Getting across the Dnieper was tricky, but his fluent Russian helped him bluff his way. "I left my wife, alone, with three small children, one a little baby," he said. "I want to get them and bring them to safety." Amazingly, the soldiers let him cross the river. Now that Isaac was home again, he had to go into hiding. If the communists found him, he would be shot.

Leave Nothing For The Germans!

In the village, pandemonium reigned. In an impassioned speech on Radio Moscow, Stalin commanded, "Defend your country! Do not leave anything for the Germans, whether a machine, an animal, or a sack of grain... Evacuate every kolkhoz, every village." All day soldiers and jeeps moved west to fight the Germans. In the evening and at night, large herds of cows were herded past our house, their full udders causing them much discomfort. The herdsmen called for us women to milk the cows. We milked as many as we could, but we could not milk them all. Hundreds upon hundreds of cows were left to endure their painfully engorged udders. At night I couldn't sleep for the cows distressful bawling. Then herds of sheep, pigs and horses followed. The herdsmen couldn't control the animals, nor could the narrow street contain them. They surged into our yards trampling down our carefully tended gardens. After the kolkhoz barns and stables were emptied, our own animals were rounded up. One morning all our sheep were driven east across the Dnieper, accompanied by their shepherds; Isaac's twelve-year-old brother Hans was among them. Because the day promised to be a hot one, Hans had gone barefoot, wearing a short-sleeved shirt and shorts. Now his mother reproached herself bitterly, "If only I had insisted on warmer clothing and shoes and packed him a better lunch," she whimpered. "What will become of my boy?" (Hans never did return. Most of the Germans who crossed the river were sent to Siberia. They were considered suspect and the Russians wanted them out of the way.)

One day we heard, "They're rounding up our cows to take them across the Dnieper."

Hurriedly I joined a group of determined women heading for the pasture with ropes in hand. Ignoring the men on horseback, we dashed among the herd in search of our cows. We would take them home with us immediately.

"Women are you crazy?" a man shouted.

"We want our cows to come home."

"You'll get your cows on the other side of the Dnieper."

"We want them now. Our children need milk."

The man cracked his whip in the air, but he didn't actually hit us. Was he bluffing? Perhaps he was thinking of his own little children needing milk. Maybe he was amused at the women's spunk. At any rate, we got our cows back. For the rest of the evacuation, we did not let our cows out of the barns again. The same thing happened in a nearby town, but the woman who organized the protest was arrested and shipped off to Siberia. It was always dangerous to oppose the state.

Early one morning as I was going to the barn to milk the cow, the earth trembled under my feet. A distant rumble became louder. I looked west towards the hills. Horses, hundreds of them, crested the hill and thundered down into our village. As in a dream, I stood transfixed. Beautiful Arabian horses, in glorious perfection, surged past me, wave upon wave. They streaked through our village and up the road to Chortitza. The kolkhoz stables in Bes Arabia had been emptied.

The Dnieper River became one seething mass of frightened animals. Many clambered onto the Chortitza Island, but it, too, became choked. Strong animals swam across to the other shore, but many animals drowned and the shores became littered with dead animals. This made me very sad. In this evil war, why did animals have to lose their lives?

Day after day, wagons filled with refugees fleeing east, rumbled through our village. Some said they were Jewish and were escaping Nazi Germany. This puzzled me greatly, for I didn't have the slightest inkling of what was going on there. *Why would anybody go into Russia of their own free will?* I wondered. Soon an edict came for all inhabitants of Neuendorf to evacuate and head east across the Dnieper. We were to leave that very evening, but I refused to pack. After supper, like on all other evenings, I simply put the children to bed.

"Neta, be sensible," my husband said.

"I'm not going,"

"We'll be shot."

"They can shoot me then."

"Think of our children."

"Either way they're doomed," I began to cry. "You know the communists. They'll send you to the front; I'll be sent to Siberia, and the children?" I began to sob hysterically. "The children...will be shipped away...to an orphanage."

I couldn't control my sobbing. Isaac walked from room to room, deeply agitated.

"Maybe there's a way," he muttered. "I'll see Klassen."

An hour later, he returned. "We're going to attempt an escape. Klassen has a wagon. Pack some food. I'll get the rest ready."

We Hide In Grain Fields

Just after dark, a wagon rumbled onto our yard. "Everything into the wagon," Isaac whispered. He lifted Lena from her bed and hoisted her into the wagon. I followed with Agnes in my arms. Then Isaac went back to get

Fred. Beside the Klassens' seven children, we bedded down our three and spread a quilt over them all. While Isaac packed our few belongings into the wagon, I brought our cow from the barn and tied her onto the back of the wagon beside the Klassen's cow.

It was dark and overcast. No moon shone tonight. An eery feeling made us trudge along beside the wagon in silence. Most wagons would be rumbling east this night. We had chosen to go west towards the approaching German army. It was a dangerous move, but we thought we had a better chance with them than the Russians. How long before somebody got suspicious?

In a corn field, we heard rustling, then voices. We froze, straining to hear the words. "They're speaking platt deutsch," Isaac whispered. Relief washed over us; they were escapees like ourselves. It made us feel better. We thought we were the only ones fleeing the Russians.

The road was jammed with Russian soldiers, some on horses, some on foot, retreating from the German army. One barked at my husband, "*Stoi!* Stop! What are you hauling in that wagon?"

"Children."

The soldier yanked the blanket off the children. Startled awake, some began to cry. "Oh, my God," he said, "Where are you going?"

"We're from Krievarog," my husband lied. "We're fleeing from the German enemy."

"Not this way," the soldier shook his head. "Turn around."

The soldiers watched our men turn the horses and wagon around and accompanied us for a short distance, but they became impatient at our slow rate of travel. They shouted a warning, then rode off into the night. Quickly, our men redirected the wagon and we rolled west again.

Soon we were confronted with another group of Russian soldiers. Again, we had to turn horses and wagon around. The third time it happened, Isaac feigned wagon trouble. "All the good wagons are used in the army," he complained. "How can we possibly make better progress?"

"Let's take them along," one soldier said.

They must have thought it too much trouble for they, too, rode off.

Once the road was clear, Klassen turned the wagon west again and left the road. All night we bumped across the fields, avoiding the highway. It was just too risky.

By morning, we came to a valley where we decided to spend the day. Katarina Klassen and I milked our cows, then turned them loose to graze. The horses, likewise, were set free to graze. It was a beautiful August morning. Birds warbled in the trees. A slight breeze stirred. We served our children bread and milk for breakfast. All day they played together beautifully. Little Fred who was still weak from his illness sat on the warm grass and played contentedly with his teddy bear. His cheeks had a healthy glow on them. *How fortunate children are*, I thought. *They don't know the danger they're in.*

Meanwhile, Isaac and Klassen tried to sneak into a village to replenish our empty water containers and snatch some news of the war. They found the village almost entirely deserted; only a few people remained. So as to avoid suspicion, they didn't ask too many questions. Quickly they refilled their containers at a well and returned.

All through the next night we travelled west along the wagon trails between fields of corn and grain. By the second morning, we arrived at a big wheat field bordering a highway. Many army trucks and tanks rolled east—Russian or German? We couldn't tell; they were too far away.

Once darkness fell, our men crept up to the highway. "They're German!" Isaac whispered to Klassen. The men kept under cover until they reached a village brimming with German military personnel. Isaac walked up to a group of soldiers and surprised them by addressing them in their native tongue. They hadn't expected to find German people living in Russia. A couple of hours later, our men returned accompanied by German soldiers. I don't know who was more surprised, us or them. The soldiers smiled when our children spoke German to them. "So far into Russia we find German-speaking people." They shook their heads.

"Our ancestors came from Prussia—over one hundred fifty years ago," Isaac explained.

"But we've always been proud of our heritage. We've kept our language and our customs."

"Wunderbar!" they kept saying.

I could see Isaac was making quite an impression on them. "Join the army," one of them said. "With your knowledge of Ukrainian and Russian, you could be useful to us."

"My family needs me," Isaac said.

The soldiers advised us not to return home immediately for there was still too much military action. On the third day, we returned home using the highway. Army trucks full of German soldiers rumbled past us. All along the road we saw dead animals that had succumbed during those frantic cattle drives. Some carcasses had been covered with sheaves. I wanted to cry.

All of Neuendorf buzzed with German jeeps and soldiers and wagons of people returning from hiding. The Krökers were already home. They had also been in hiding, but not so far from home. On our yard stood a German Red Cross jeep.

Much relieved, we moved back into our familiar home. Surely God had protected us in our flight and brought us home safely. Some German soldiers billeted with us. They were kind men who reminded me of my brothers. They took our children on their knees and taught them little songs, or told them a Brother Grimm's fairy tale. "This war will soon be over," they said. I hoped they were right. I wanted to forget the terrible hardships suffered under communism and begin to build a more secure future for our children. But hope, based on man's ideology, can be easily dashed. How soon we were to find this out.

Russian Counterattack

One day, the children and I were eating lunch. Isaac was away working. Suddenly, a loud explosion shook the whole house. More explosions followed. The windows and door rattled. Bits of plaster from the ceiling covered our food. Dust and smoke swirled past the window; chunks of debris sailed past. I grabbed the smallest two children and dashed into the cellar, yelling for Lena to follow. She mustn't have heard me, for she didn't come. In the confusion and the deafening noise of an air raid, we became separated. Thus, my five-year-old found herself all alone amidst the chaos. She ran into the kitchen calling for me and bumped into soldiers lying on their stomachs. "Lie down," they shouted. One soldier grabbed her and pushed her down. "I want my mommy," she whimpered.

"Not now," he ordered. "Lie still."

When I returned to the house, the soldier brought Lena to me.

"Next time, do a head count," he said.

I looked down at the floor. *He must think I'm a terrible mother.* Truth is, I never could get over the fright of an air raid. With the first explosion, all reason left me. Sometimes, instead of getting myself and my children to safety, I'd make a dash for the barn to see if my cow was alright.

When I went outside to survey the damage, I saw a crater where a bomb had exploded in the neighbour's garden. Shrapnel lay scattered across our yard. A woman and a small boy had been killed. Medics brought a wounded soldier to our house on a stretcher. Blood oozed through his uniform and dripped onto the floor. He kept calling, "Help me! Please, help me." Hurriedly I brought some hot water and clean rags from the kitchen. Although I told Lena to go away, she was mesmerized by the whole scene, almost like she wanted to be near the man to comfort him. (Lena grew up to become a nurse. I believe, her interest in nursing was born during this time.)

I was eager to find out how my family had fared during the evacuation, so on the following Sunday, Isaac and I, with our children, made a trip to Nieder-Chortitza. Evidence of a flood was everywhere. The Russians had blown up the dam and half of the village had flooded, but my family was safe. "Instead of going east across the Dnieper as the Russians commanded us to do, we hid in grandmas' house," Tante Anna explained. "There were thirty of us total: besides our family, there were all the relatives that live with grandmother on a steady basis, as well as some neighbours. During the day, all of us women and children crowded into the cellar and at night we hid in the house. The shutters were always closed and there was a padlock on the door making the house look deserted. One day, while we were crouching quietly in the dark house, we heard some Russian men talking just outside the window. One of them said, 'Yes, they're gone. The house is empty.' Just then a child started to cry. Aghast, the mother slapped a hand over the baby's mouth. We waited for an angry voice to command us to open the door. But no! The men walked away as though they hadn't heard a thing." My aunt stopped her narration, overcome with emotion. "God was so obviously with us," she said. "I believe He made them deaf so they couldn't hear us.

"Very early on the morning of August 18, 1941, we heard traffic moving past the house," my aunt continued. "I said to Tina, 'Let's go and see what's happening.' We crept along the lilac hedge which was between Grandmother's house and the road, and peeked out. There were jeeps with trees on top and many soldiers in German uniform. We heard one soldier saying, '*Ja, die Richtung stimmt.*' (The orientation is right.) Apparently the day before, two German soldiers in civilian clothing had scouted out the town. Now, as they were leading their battalion into town, they were somewhat confused because of the flooding. Hence the comment: '*Gestern war doch kein Wasser, aber die Richtung stimmt.*' (Yesterday there was no water, but the orientation is right.)

"Tina and I came out of hiding and addressed the soldiers in their native language. 'Ladies, what are you doing here?' one soldier exclaimed. They were clearly delighted to meet German-speaking people so far into Russia. They told us to go back into the house, because there were still Russian soldiers about and it wasn't safe to come out of hiding."

Visiting my family, gave me great comfort. The women were safe at the moment, but I wondered what had happened to my brothers. I learned that Peter had gone east with his tractor brigade and not been heard of again. My brother, Henry, had been sent to Siberia during Stalin's purges. Only Gerhard who was teaching in Odessa, seemed to be safe. I didn't know then that Peter and Gerhard would also spend many years in Siberian labour camps. I would not see my brothers again for almost forty years.

CHAPTER SIX

German Occupation (1941-1943)

THE RUSSIAN COUNTER-ATTACK signalled the first
of many air strikes. Soon wrecks of bombed jeeps scattered the village and countryside. Isaac collected useful parts
and constructed an automobile. In one month, he had it
completed. Though it was oddly shaped, it worked well. I
was very proud of him. But the Germans took it away from
him. "No civilian is allowed to own a car," they said. Isaac
received a promissory note that it would be returned to him
after the war. We were used to confiscations. The Russians
had taken away our motorcycle, radio, and bicycles and not
returned them. Would the Germans deliver?

One German soldier kept taking photos of Fred.
Although our son was now stronger, he still looked emaciated. I wondered what he wanted with my son's photo.

"We're doing a report on the children in Russia," he
said.

"Why not use photos of my girls?" I was annoyed.

"*Schon gut,*" he said. (Never mind.) But I did mind. I
didn't want my child's photo used for Nazi propaganda.

Furthermore, it was an unfair representation of children in Russia to photograph only a thin child.

To feed their armed forces the Germans instituted a tax system: there was a milk plan, an egg plan, a meat plan, and a bread plan. Much of the grain had been trampled by stampeding horses and cows, but we salvaged what we could. We harvested our orchards and dried the fruit; we canned vegetables from our gardens. Since coal was impossible to get, we cooked and heated our houses with straw and dried maize cobs and sunflower stalks. We were thankful that our brick ovens, designed to hold heat for hours, required only a minimum amount of fuel. Soon there was total food rationing. We didn't mind sharing our food with the Germans for they treated us kindly and restored some of the freedoms we had lost under communism.

In the fall, German schools were organized using our own Mennonite teachers. My two sisters, Tina and Annie, taught kindergarten in Nieder-Chortitza and my brother, Gerhard, taught school in Odessa. Churches, closed for years under the communists, were reopened. The buildings were cleaned, and benches and a pulpit were put in place. Once more people flocked to our church to worship God in public. But we had no Bibles or song books. They had been destroyed in Stalin's purges.

Once more on Christmas Eve, people streamed to the stately church building in Neuendorf for the annual Christmas Eve program. Among them were a good number of German soldiers who seemed to be as excited as we were.

Soon the church was filled. I took a deep breath of the pungent smell of evergreen and burning candle wax. Had a Christmas tree ever looked more radiant? As I listened to the congregation singing in four-part harmony the old familiar Christmas carols, my heart swelled with gratitude to God. Surely He had sent the Germans to deliver us and restore to us our freedom. For once, I could look forward to the future with hope.

Since all the farm machinery had been taken by the Russians, Isaac's job as machinist became obsolete. The Germans asked my husband to work for them as chauffer and interpreter. At first Isaac refused, but later he and four other young men from his tractor brigade relented and accepted the offer. I've been asked why my husband, a Mennonite who believed in pacifism, would go to work for the German military. The main reason was that he needed a job to feed his growing family. Moreover, our people had suffered incredible hardships and losses under communism. We had prayed fervently that God would deliver us. Now it seemed that God had indeed heard our prayers. Hadn't He sent the German soldiers to be our liberators from Stalin's oppressive regime? Of course, we knew nothing about the Nazi ideology or the persecution of the Jews. Mennonite young men who worked for the German military as interpreters and chauffeurs probably felt that with the German blitzkrieg tactic, the war would soon be over and they would never see the fighting front. But it was a grave miscalculation.

Isaac Is Drafted Into The German Army

One day, Isaac came home wearing a German uniform just like I had seen five other men from Neuendorf doing.

"What does this mean?" I asked alarmed.

"I'm now officially drafted." He looked dismayed.

"But they'll send you to the front."

"Neta, I'm an interpreter and chauffeur. They don't want me fighting."

But I had my doubts. The Germans scorned the Mennonite's belief in pacifism. To serve the Fatherland and help build their Reich was a high honour, they said. Would they be satisfied to let our men dig trenches and drive jeeps?

With a heavy heart, I consulted with the other wives whose husbands had been drafted. *What can we do to save our men?* we wondered. After much discussion we decided that all six of us would travel to Zaporozhye, the nearest Russian city, and appeal to the superintendent of the German army.

An officer in immaculate grey-green uniform smiled benignly at the motley group of peasant women in his office. "Ladies, what can I do for you?"

"We want our men to come home."

He leaned back in his chair. "Let me get this straight, you want me to release your men from the German army?"

"Yes, our children are small and they need their fathers."

"But that's clearly impossible," he stated with mock horror. "We need your men to help us win this war." He rubbed his hands together as though he could already taste victory. "This war will soon be over, and your men will return as heroes."

"We need our men now."

"Of course, you need help," the officer said amiably. "I'll see to it that you get some."

But the promised help never came.

In fact, soon more and more men, young and old, were conscripted to dig trenches and help the war effort.

As winter approached and icy winds raked across the Ukrainian steppes, German soldiers in light summer uniforms and footwear kept pouring through Neuendorf on their way to the front.

"Don't you have winter uniforms?" I asked.

"Oh, Mama, we'll soon be snug and warm in Moscow and Stalingrad," a soldier laughed. He explained that the blitzkrieg tactic enabled them to spend winters in captured cities. Such confidence was reassuring for Isaac's sake, but still, I thought it very audacious.

As the German army advanced further east, Isaac moved with them. Now we didn't see him for months on end. Eagerly, I devoured his letters when they arrived.

Ostfront, February 1942

Dear Neta,

My thoughts are constantly with you and the children. As passionately as we in Russia long for spring, I wait for a letter from you. Please write me more often. Write me how you manage all the work. Soon it will be warm enough to plant a garden. Plant as much as you can for I can't promise you much financial help. My wage is so low, and the little I do save, I can't even send you.

Peter Thiessen tells me you are to become Reichsdeutsche. (Citizens of the Third Reich). Neta, don't rush into this. Better leave it for now. I have my reasons for saying this, but I would rather not put them on paper.

Don't worry about me, Neta. In my 28 years I have survived many hardships, and I'll survive this one too. Take care of yourself and the children. Remember, behind the dark clouds the sun is shining and it will

shine for us again. Never lose heart! One more thing,
Neta. Please don't give away my tools. When I return
I shall need them. Let's hope it's soon.

With much love, Isaac

A House For A Cow And A Pig

Isaac and I had often talked about building our own
house, but he had always been too busy. Besides, there was
no building material available. One day, I heard of a good
house for sale. The asking price? A cow and a fattened
pig.

Should I buy it? I hated doing such a big business
transaction without consulting Isaac. Besides, what would
we eat if I gave away our source of food? Some people
advised me, "If you want a house so badly, move into one
of the vacant ones." (Some homes had been left abandoned
by families that had gone east across the Dnieper with the
Russians.) *But those houses don't belong to me*, I thought. *I*
want one that's really mine. After several sleepless nights, I
bought the house.

But when I saw my children eating dry bread and
potatoes the rest of the winter, guilt set in. Why had I given
away our only source of milk, butter and meat? When the
children went across the street to their grandmother's house,
she would put butter on their bread and give them milk to
drink. A real treat that winter! Finally spring came. I planted
fruit trees: apple, cherry, plum, and apricots. I made a large
garden and planted potatoes, beans, carrots, cucumbers and
sugar beets.

One sunny April morning after chores and before the
children were awake, I was on my usual inspection tour of
the yard and the garden. I loved to personally greet every
new shoot that came up. What would Isaac say about these

uneven rows in my garden? I chuckled. He always teased me about not being able to make a straight line. Pictures on the wall that hung crooked, rows not quite parallel, or bread slices thicker at one end than the other bothered him. "Can't you see that's not straight?" he'd ask good-naturedly. An intense longing to see him again welled up inside me and tears watered the soil as I yanked out weeds. *When will this war be over?*

Suddenly, I heard footsteps approaching. Sure, steady, deliberate steps that neared our yard. I looked up and thought I saw a ghost. Isaac, so handsome in his uniform and shiny boots, came towards me. The next instant I was in my husband's arms.

"You look great, Neta," he beamed. "All the hardships haven't spoiled your good looks."

I grinned. I had so much to tell him, and now that he actually stood before me, my mind was blank.

"What's all this?" Isaac waved his hand across our yard and towards the house. "I hear rumours."

"Oh, Isaac, wait until I show you," I said.

"First, I want to see the children," he laughed. "Do you think they'll still recognize me?"

At first, the children acted strange toward their father but soon they warmed up to him. He coaxed the girls to come and receive a gift, then he took Fred onto his lap. For two weeks we were a family reunited.

Eagerly, I showed Isaac our new home. At first, he feigned indifference: I shouldn't have given away the children's food, he said. A house could have waited. But later he warmed up to the idea of having our own property and he spoke animatedly about how he would fix it up after the war. He praised me for making a big garden and orchard. "With the money I brought home, you can buy another cow and piglet," he said.

During the time Isaac was home, he went to the German headquarters in Chortitza requesting a discharge for religious reasons, but the officer merely laughed at him. After his two-week furlough and a tearful goodbye, Isaac left for the front again.

In August, when the Germans advanced into the Caucasus, a region between the Black sea and the Caspian sea, Isaac was among them.

Meanwhile, back in our villages we tried to bring the harvest in. To replace the communist's kolkhoz, groups of field workers were formed. These groups were comprised mostly of women. Many of our men were lost in Stalin's purges and in the Russian evacuation, and the German army had conscripted others. In the morning, after chores were done and the children had been taken to Grandmother Loewen's house, Isaac's sister and I joined a group of women equipped with spades, hoes, and rakes heading towards the fields outside Neuendorf. We worked all day. I forced myself to ignore the nausea and overwhelming tiredness of another pregnancy. If we wanted to eat next winter, I couldn't afford to be sick.

Letters from Isaac came with amazing regularity. In one letter, he wrote:

Ostfront, September 1942

Dear Neta,

We are again out of immediate danger, but many sleepless nights are behind us.

Neta, don't be hurt if you don't receive more letters from me, but when you are running it isn't possible to write. Mother wrote that you are hurt that I'm not sending you parcels like my brother Peter sends to his wife. Remember, my dearest, that I am not in Italy

like he is, but in desolate parts of Russia. No, I haven't forgotten you, even if Mother thinks I have. Twice I have applied for leave to come home, but it isn't so easy to get it. But the time will come when I can be home caring for you again.
Auf wiedersehen and write soon.
Isaac

On Furlough

On November 5, 1942 Isaac came home on furlough. The three marvellous days together went all too quickly and all too soon I watched him dress in his immaculate uniform and prepare to leave. I begged him to stay home, but he said he had to go.

Reluctantly, I buttoned my heavy winter coat over my bulging stomach, seven months pregnant, and put on some Russian felt boots. A vicious wind rattled the house and Isaac said, "You're not going out in this."

"I want to walk you to the depot," I said.

"In your condition?" His soft, grey eyes reflected his worry.

"I'm all right."

We trudged through the deep snow together. An icy wind tore at us and stung our faces. After a short distance, Isaac stopped and urged, "Neta, go back now."

"No, I'm okay." Stubbornly, I clung to his arm.

A compulsion to hold him back—to hide him from the Germans and all who wanted to snatch him away—drove me on. Dread filled me that if I let go of him, I would never see him again. He'd be lost to me forever. So I hung on fiercely as though somehow I could prevent his going away.

Several times we stopped so I could get my breath and Isaac worried about missing his train. He faced me tall and handsome, with eyes full of tenderness. "Neta, write often. Write—about the baby." He held me for a few minutes, kissed me, and then walked briskly away.

You will never see him again. I heard the words as clearly as if they had been spoken. Was it my imagination or a premonition? I didn't know, but many times in the months and years ahead, I would think of this ominous message. For that *was* the last time I saw Isaac. I can still picture him walking away through the deep snow with suitcase in hand.

Katie Is Born

During the winter months, hundreds of refugees from the Volga district and the Caucasus filled Neuendorf and were billeted in our homes. Their stories were grim and filled with descriptions of dead uniformed bodies, carcasses of horses, broken aircraft, and bombed machinery littering the frozen steppes. Russian troops, better prepared to fight in winter, made remarkable advances while the German army suffered terrible losses.

Neuendorf swelled with refugees and wounded German soldiers. In our home, one soldier slept on a bench, another one slept on the sofa.

After midnight on January 24, 1943, I awoke with labour pains. I waited until 4 a.m., then I dressed and stepped out into the cold, swirling snow. It was dark as I trudged to Mother's house and knocked on her bedroom window.

"Who's there?" she called.

"Me. Neta. I'm going now—"

"Wait, Lena can go with you," Mother shouted.

"No, let her sleep," I said.

I pushed into the restraining wind. Where was the road to the midwife's house? Deep snow drifts covered everything and it was hard to tell. A strong labour pain seized me. I doubled over and clung to a fence post. *I must follow this fence*, I kept saying to myself. My legs sank deep into the snow, over my knees. I kept willing my legs to move forward pausing only for contractions as they came. As my labour pains increased, my groans mingled with the screaming wind. How much further? Two kilometres never were this long before. Finally, the midwife's house loomed out of the swirling whiteness.

Quickly the midwife (her name was Anna Schmidt, Isaac's cousin) pulled me into her house and told me to sit down. Then she tried to coax a fire in the stove, but the wet wood sizzled and smouldered. Because fuel was so scarce, she did not heat the birthing room unless she had a patient in it. I don't know which was worse, the labour pains or the fierce cold.

At nine o'clock, my daughter was born. Finally, I could snuggle into bed under a warm feather quilt. Soon I fell sound asleep. It seemed only moments later when somebody woke me. I opened my eyes and saw Katie Tschetter, Isaac's cousin, smiling down at me. "I've brought you some chicken noodle soup," she said. My absolute favourite food!

"Now I know what I'll name my daughter," I exclaimed. "I'll call her Katie, after you."

When I returned home two weeks later with my baby daughter, I found a very full house. More soldiers had moved in, also a refugee woman from the Caucasus. At first, Isaac's sister helped me cook for them all, but then she returned home to help Mother whose house was full also. Then I became ill, and Lena had to help me again. Our biggest problem was getting enough water for so many people. We had no well and every pailful had to be carried from Mother's house across the street. While I was gone, our cow had had a calf. Now we had enough milk for us all.

With so many people in the house other problems arose. The soldiers often forgot to close the door behind themselves, causing a terrible draft. Soon my two-month-old baby developed pneumonia. Her little chest wheezed to get enough air and her mouth and finger nails became dusky. Not being able to suck, she whimpered pitifully. I spooned warm milk into her mouth, but worried that she wasn't getting enough to eat.

Meanwhile, the refugee woman from Caucasus staying with us watched me. Perhaps it was Katie's pitiful cries that made her say, "Frau Loewen, let her die. She'll be better off."

I stared at her bleakly.

"Think about it. You'll soon be on the road," she said, her face becoming flushed. "Children die on the road and nobody has time to bury them." She mopped her forehead as though trying to wipe away a terrible memory. "Put her out of her suffering."

Not believing my ears, I continued to stare at her flushed face.

"Put her outside," her dark eyes shone fiercely, "It's cold enough. A few minutes and it'll be over."

Suddenly, the full impact of what she was saying hit me. "You devil!" I screamed. "Get out of my house!"

Clutching Katie to my breast, I fled to the cold bedroom. The raging turmoil in my chest made me gasp for breath. I felt myself being sucked into a black whirlpool of helplessness. "Oh God, help!" I moaned. "Have mercy on us."

Eventually, the storm in my chest beat itself out and a deep quiet filled me. "God, You are with me and You have heard me," I whispered. I looked down at my child's dusky face, "Katie, you will live. I know you will."

When I came back into the kitchen, the woman was gone.

Letters From Isaac

Letters from Isaac both cheered and puzzled me. Although I wrote him every week, it was evident that my letters were not getting through to him.

Ostfront, February 1943

Dear Neta,
Have you had the baby yet? If so, what do we have, boy or girl? What did you name the baby? How are you managing, Neta? Did you receive any money from the German commissioners? I have saved 163 rubles. If only I had a way of mailing it to you, it would help you a little. Did you receive enough coal and wheat? I hope the Germans do better with the distribution of that than they did with the clothes. Is the house warm enough so the children don't catch cold? Don't lose heart, Neta. Remember, at the end of winter May is sure to come.

Ostfront, March 1943

Dear Neta,
I spent all of January and half of February outside, mostly on horseback, not only days but also nights. I got to know from which direction the wind was blowing! For the past three days we've been stationed at one place so I can finally write you a letter. My thoughts are constantly with you and the children. I keep wondering how you've managed all winter.
Was Lena able to attend school? Is Agnes in good health? And Fred, is he walking on sturdy little legs again? And the baby? I haven't heard any news yet.

Ostfront, April 1943

Dear Neta,

At long last I received some news from you. So we have a healthy baby girl and all went well at her birth. Thank God for that!

I am well too, Neta, and now that I have a letter from you, I feel considerably cheered up. It gives me great joy to know you were able to give the children a little happiness at Christmas.

Neta, it is sad for us Russian-born German soldiers. We have lived 165 years in Russia and despite great hardships, we have kept our German language and culture, and now the German officers treat us like Russian peasants.

CHAPTER SEVEN

Evacuation of Neuendorf

THE SUMMER SUN ripened the fruit on the trees and the melons in the fields. Vegetables grew in abundance in the gardens. In the fields outside of Neuendorf, winter wheat stood high and green with well-formed ears. *Would any of it be for us?* we wondered sadly.

As the Russians advanced, heavy fighting pounded Zaporozhye again. We could hear the machine guns in the distance. Bombers roared overhead and sent me trembling into the house. Large search lights raked the night sky and explosions jolted us from our beds. With every day, tension in our village mounted. Leaflets fluttered from aeroplanes. "Prepare to evacuate," I read. "The German army will escort you. After the war you will be given houses and farms like the ones you are leaving behind." I didn't want to leave, but even more, I didn't want to stay behind if the Russians were coming back. The children were so young: Lena was seven; Agnes, five; Fred, three; and Katie, just 8 months old. In the midst of all this confusion another letter from Isaac reached me.

Ostfront, September 1943

Dear Neta,
We are again out of immediate danger but we've been running constantly. Neta, I worry about you. Should you have to evacuate how will you manage with four small children? Let's hope it won't come to that, but be prepared. Please write me as soon as you can and let me know exactly how and where you are. Send the letter along with a soldier going to the eastern front. I'll get it all right. Let's trust that our heavenly Father will send us only what's good for us, for without Him we can do nothing. Greet Mother and all my siblings from me. I greet you with a kiss. Good night! With much love and hoping for a happy reunion soon, Isaac

In October 1943, an evacuation order came.

My mother-in-law and I decided to butcher a pig so we'd have some meat for the journey. She asked a German soldier to shoot the pig and then we skinned it. The two of us worked hard all day. We made sausages and salted down pork. Once a mortar shell whizzed across the yard narrowly missing Mother. The next day we baked bread. Then it was time to pack. While Lena and Agnes held open the sacks, I stuffed in our clothes and blankets. In another sack, I poured in dried beans, some loaves of bread, and sausages wrapped in newspaper. I grabbed my hand-cranked Singer sewing machine and packed Isaac's letters, some photos, birth certificates, and other important papers into the casing under the gear shift.

I couldn't sleep all night. My mind raced with anxiety over our trip. Besides, the groans coming from a wounded soldier sleeping on the sofa tore at my heart. Who would look after him when I was gone? In the early morning hours, his moaning ceased. I went to check on him. Gently, I turned him over and looked into his rigid face. "Poor boy," I whispered and said a prayer for his family. Early in the morning, I woke up the children, dressed them warmly, then gave them breakfast. I surveyed the emergency equipment piled by the door. What else should I take along? Then I saw Isaac's fur coat and threw it on top of the pile. Since there would be nobody to feed the animals, I ran to the barn and untied the cow and opened the chicken coop so the animals could fend for themselves. I filled a barrel and a basin with drinking water. "God watch over you," I whispered to the animals.

An army jeep drove onto the yard; a soldier jumped out, and helped me load up. As the jeep edged towards the road, I turned for one last look at our home. What I saw made me heart-sick. Two Russian women were carrying out my baby's cradle laden with pots and pans and other kitchen utensils. A third woman carried away my spinning wheel. It hurt to see other people gloat in our misfortune. True, since we were fleeing we couldn't take those things along, but I wished they had waited until we were gone.

At the train station our stuff was unloaded, then the jeep returned for another family. What bedlam! Hundreds of people spilled out of army jeeps onto the platform. Piles of gunny sacks, boxes, and other luggage littered the station. The whole village was on the move trying to stay ahead of the advancing Russian army. If the Russians caught up with us, our future would be grim.

All day we waited in vain for a train. At night, a cold wind blew. The children laid down on top of our luggage; I covered them with my husband's fur coat, and soon they were asleep. But sleep was out of the question for me. Fighter planes flew overhead. *What if they strafe the station?* We waited another full day. We saw some air battles very near us: it was terrible to watch. Finally, the third day, the train arrived. Quickly, our luggage was loaded into boxcars and we climbed on top of it. Then we waited—another whole day that seemed like a week—while bombers screeched overhead. The longer we waited, the more my panic mounted. Would we get out of here alive?

Finally, the train lurched. It began to move slowly.

"We're going!" I cried. "We're going."

On that memorable day of October 18, 1943, I gazed out of the open door at the familiar houses and gardens moving past. Would I ever see my village again?

During the nine-day journey, we had enough food to eat, but soon we ran out of drinking water. Sometimes the train stopped at a lake. When the heavy doors were opened, everybody dashed to the shore and refilled their water containers. But the water wasn't safe for drinking. Soon our children had diarrhea. I had only three diapers for Katie and I used them up before the day was half done; then I used newspapers. But soon the papers were used up too. What a problem!

One day, Lena called from the open door, "Mommy, come look. Real live Christmas trees! Lots of them." Back home on the steppes, she had never seen evergreens growing in the countryside. The only evergreen she knew was the annual Christmas tree in the school.

After a week, we arrived in Litzmannstadt (Lodz), Poland. Army trucks transported us refugees to a large building. Behind a small table an officer filled out a paper with our names, ages, and places of birth. Then a woman, also in uniform, directed me to follow the women and children walking down a hall to the left. I noticed that men and older boys walked down a hall to the right. At a large door, a uniformed woman said, "Before you enter the shower room, you must undress the children and yourself. Leave your clothes here at the door." I looked at her dubiously. *Undress in front of complete strangers, children and adults alike?* "Don't worry, you'll get your clothes back," she said. "After they're treated."

My girls looked miserably embarrassed standing naked beside the door. My own cheeks burnt with humiliation as I began to strip. Naked, we entered a steaming large room; warm water gushed from many shower heads in the ceiling. My girls and little Fred seemed totally bewildered by the spectacle of nude bodies, every shape and form, milling about under the shower heads. But it *was* good to bathe and wash our hair after being shut up in a cattle car all week. A short while later, our clothes —which had been baked—arrived in neat bundles. But the bundles were all mixed up and, in my naked state, I had to sort through the pile until I found them. Quickly I dressed, then I helped Fred and Katie put their clothes on. Then all of us, scrubbed and in clean clothes, went into a large mess hall and received a good meal. Trucks transported us back to the train and we continued our journey west.

Gerhard and Anganetha Dyck, Neta's parents

Neta's baptism class, Pentecost Sunday, 1931. Neta is the fourth from the right,
second to the last row. Pastor Aaron Toews, who conducted the baptism,
was later arrested and banned to Siberia.

Anganetha Dyck (Neta, for short) married Isaac Loewen on June 2, 1935,
the last day of official services in the church.

The Neuendorf Mennonite Church, Ukraine, The communists closed the church
on June 3, 1935 and converted it into a Soviet granary.

Isaac and Neta on a motorcycle, the first in Neuendorf. Isaac attempted to teach his wife how to ride it, but her first and last solo attempt ended up in a collision with a garden fence.

Isaac and Neta with their three children, Fred (on Neta's lap), Lena, and Agnes. The radio, motorcycle, and bicycle were later confiscated by the communists.

Helena Loewen holding a bouquet of flowers, with Neta and
her four children. This would be our last photo together.
From left to right: Agnes, Katie (on Neta's lap), Fred and Lena

Isaac worked as a machinist and later as leader of his brigade in the *kolkhoz*.
He's sitting on the tractor in front.

PART TWO

A Refugee in Europe (1943-1949)

CHAPTER EIGHT

Refugee Camp in Kulm, Poland (1943)

T HE FOLLOWING EVENING we arrived in Kulm (Chelmno). "Everybody out," a conductor said. When I disembarked with my children, I saw my neighbours from Neuendorf, Ukraine, and took comfort. Even in this strange land, I was surrounded by neighbours, relatives, and acquaintances. It was a reassuring sight. A woman in uniform approached me and said, "I'll take your baby now."

Bewildered, I said, "No, thank you. I'll carry her."

"You'll come later with your luggage," she said. "I'll take your baby now."

I didn't understand. "Where are you going with my child?"

"To a nursery." Seeing the disquiet on my face, she added, "Don't worry, you'll be at the same refugee camp." I reluctantly handed Katie over.

We entered rows upon rows of barracks. At an office we registered and were given ration cards. Then we found the room allocated to us. Isaac's mother, sister Lena, and I, with my three children shared one room with two bunk beds. We were very cramped and I worried that my children might get on Mother's nerves because she didn't have much patience.

I also worried about Katie, my nine-month-old in the nursery; she'd never been separated from me before. How was she getting on? I was still nursing her. So, early the next morning, I hurried towards the nursery barrack, which was easily identified by the crying of many babies. Other mothers, eager to feed their infants, crowded the doorway, but a large woman in uniform barred the door.

"Your babies are being bottle fed," she said.

"But that's unnecessary. We've come to feed them."

"In Germany we do things differently," the nurse said. "We're a bit more civilized than you were in Russia." She turned to go inside.

"I want to feed my baby," I said stubbornly.

"Yes, that's what we've come for," the women chorused. We did not stop pestering the nurse until she gave us our babies. We hugged our babies to our breasts, sat down on the grass, and relished the intimacy with our children. The nurse looked at us with disgust, "Just like a herd of cows," she said and walked inside.

We mothers took turns cooking our meals on several wood stoves in a communal kitchen. The groceries supplied were enough to feed our families. That was a good thing, for without refrigeration the pork and sausages we had brought from home had spoiled.

Nights in the barracks held a special terror for us. Millions of bedbugs streamed out of the cracks in the walls to attack us. In an effort to get away from them, I pulled the mattress off the bed onto the floor, but the bedbugs found us there too. Agnes was so badly bitten that the Red Cross nurse thought she had a skin disease.

A Letter and a Dream

Soon I received a letter from Isaac.

Ostfront, November 1943

Dear Neta,

With great joy, I found out where you are and I do hope this letter reaches you. I haven't had any news of you for a long time. How did you manage to escape? What were you able to take along? Do you have enough food and clothes for the children? Are they well? Where are my mother and sister? Do you have enough money to live on?

Please write me as soon as possible. My address is Feld Post Number 47792/C. Give my letter to a soldier, I'll get it all right. You have no idea how I'm longing to hear from you. They've promised me a furlough as soon as I hear from you. I know you're as anxious to see me as I am to see you. I have some sweets for the children, also for you I have some gifts. I've wanted to send you a parcel, but I didn't know how to reach you.

Neta, I know it's not easy for you with small children in a foreign land. Don't lose hope. We'll soon be together again, and then I'll help you care for our children.

I'll see you soon. With love and a kiss, Isaac

I was overjoyed. Isaac might be with us soon—for Christmas maybe. What a gift that would be! Maybe it was the excitement of waiting for my beloved husband that made me dream of aeroplanes. One night, I dreamed that I was standing by a window watching an aeroplane flying low above the rooftops. As the plane came closer, I saw the pilot sitting at the controls. He turned his face towards me, picked up a letter, and threw it in my direction. The letter sailed through the open window and landed on my chest. Its weight surprised me—it was as heavy as though I'd been hit by a brick. Startled by the impact, I woke up. What a strange dream! What did it mean?

I didn't have long to find out. The following day, while I was preparing our meal, an announcement on the intercom startled me. "Frau Loewen, please come to the office." *Me?* I looked around to see if other women were also preparing to go, but no, I was the only one called. Whatever for?

My heart pounded as I entered the office.

A German officer met me at the door, shook my hand, and asked me to take a seat. Then he picked up a long white envelope lying on his desk and cleared his throat.

"I'm afraid I have bad news for you," he said. "Your husband has been reported missing in action." *How can that be?* I thought. *I just heard from him.* I scarcely heard the officer's explanation of a surprise tank attack by the Russians; my mind froze around one word: *missing.* Then he's not dead. He's just missing. He could still come home. *Isaac is a smart man*, I reasoned. *He'll find a way.* Like he did when he left his tractor brigade and fled across the Dnieper; or like the time when we made an escape and hid in the wheat fields. *Missing* carried the possibility of being found one day. And I was determined to cling to hope until Isaac was found.

Depression: The Blackness

But as Christmas approached and there was no further news of my husband, the frail hope I had been clinging to evaporated and a feeling of gloom, like a shroud, settled upon me. To make matters worse, Isaac's mother and sister were sent away to a farm to work. It seemed like a bad omen as even that link with my husband's family was severed. As I sank deeper and deeper into a depression, I lost my will to live. I couldn't eat; I couldn't sleep. I didn't have the energy to check on my children to see whether they were dressed warmly against the winter's cold. I didn't have the presence of mind to go to the kitchen to prepare a meal for them. Once when three-year-old Fred saw me crying he said, "Don't cry anymore, Mama. When I'm big, I'll build you a house and then I'll be Papa."

During this difficult time, Anna Harder, a friend from Neuendorf, who, along with her three children, had moved in with me proved to be an absolute God-send. Without one word of reproach, Anna took care of my children as though they were her own. Her husband, Franz, had terminal tuberculosis and was quarantined in the hospital barrack. Sometimes Anna and I wept together. My husband was missing; hers was dying of T. B. We found solace in each other's grief and often prayed together.

On Sundays, a few Mennonite families gathered in the chapel to read a portion of Scripture and to sing and pray together. But I had been too despondent to attend. Now with Anna's gentle encouragement, I began to attend worship services and to read the Bible again. But I could never sing the songs. How could I sing when my heart was breaking? As the months passed and God's gentle words trickled into my heart, I began to sense a stirring in my soul. It reminded me of our winters at home in Ukraine: a change of temperature in the air and the ice on the Dnieper would crack and shift and the frozen landscape would soften and melt. Although icy winds still chilled us to the core, we knew winter was defeated and spring was on its way. The great sadness that had burdened me for so long began to shift, as though softened by a Divine warmth.

Light Breaks Through (Easter, 1944)

On Easter Sunday, I found myself really listening to the words of the hymns the small congregation was singing: "Death cannot keep its prey, Jesus my Saviour! He tore the bars away Jesus my Lord!...He arose! He arose! Like a mighty triumph He arose!" As I savoured these words a whisper of hope stirred within: *Maybe I too can rise again.* This living Christ we sang about was still with me. He would heal my broken heart. He would give me courage to go on. I can't adequately explain what happened to me during the service, but I felt my heavy burden being lifted. It was as though Somebody came and took it off my shoulders. And I was comforted.

With every new day, hope grew. The light at the end of the tunnel got brighter. Once more I had the desire and energy to accompany my children on walks over the countryside. Sometimes we gathered flowers and bits of moss and pine cones in the forest. And sometimes, I could even join in the songs the congregation was singing. I was on the other side of the dark valley and light had broken through.

CHAPTER NINE

In Poland:
Borrowed Houses

IN JUNE 1944 we evacuated the refugee camp in Kulm.
The front was once more too close for comfort. Trains
took us as far as Wartegau, Poland. Then farmers came
with their hay wagons to take us to Dieterwald. Back in our
homeland, the Germans had promised to reimburse us for
the homes and fields we had left behind. Now in an attempt
to keep their promise, Polish people were forced to leave
their homes to make room for us refugees.

For the beautiful brick house we had left behind in
Ukraine, I was given a three-room shack poking out of a
patch of weeds. The driver unloaded our baggage by the
front door and disappeared. Feeling like an intruder, I
went inside the shack. It had a dirt floor and the walls were
blackened with soot and smoke. Stinging nettles, several feet
high, surrounded the shack. Broken window panes were
stuffed with newspaper. An old man sat dejectedly in a room
at the back. I tried to talk with him but he didn't speak a
word of German and I couldn't speak a word of Polish. I felt
sorry for the man whose house we were to share.

Not wanting to intrude, the children and I spent most of the next three days outside.

When I met the *bürgermeister* (mayor), he asked me about my husband. "He's in the German army, " I said. "He may be coming home soon." *Oh, God, let it be so.*

"My goodness," he exclaimed. "We must find you a nicer place then."

The very next morning he sent a hay wagon to transport us to a little house on an estate owned by a German couple named Kerns. As I watched an elderly Polish couple carry their belongings into the barn, I felt terrible. I didn't want a home at their expense! "Come visit me," I whispered to the woman. "You're always welcome."

The Kerns lived in a large house across the cobblestone yard. Whereas in Kulm all us Mennonite folk had lived together in one refugee camp, now we were scattered among the farmers across Poland. Only eight families from our village lived in Dieterwald; among them were Franz and Anna Harder with their children and Sarah Harder, their sister-in-law, with her seven children.

Soon Lena and Agnes were enrolled in the village school. Taking little Katie and Fred with me, I joined the Kerns' hired help culling potatoes in the barn. Working side by side with the Polish woman, we soon became good friends. I marvelled at her sweet attitude towards me; after all, it was because of me that she and her husband now lived in a curtained-off section in the barn. But when I apologized to her for living in her house, she said, "Just take good care of it. I know you're not staying long." I nodded. The Russian front was coming closer every day.

After school one day Lena asked me, "Are we Nazis?"

"Of course not!" I said. "You're a Mennonite. Why do you ask?"

"A boy called me Nazi and threw some dirt at me," she said, her blue eyes mirroring confusion.

"Don't pay him any attention," I said. "He thinks you're a Nazi because you speak German. Try to be nice to him anyway." *How cruel war is,* I thought. Innocent children who, under normal circumstances, would have great fun playing together, are made suspicious of each other, or worse, they are taught to hate one another.

Lessons In Faith

By summer, air strikes hit Lodz and Warsaw. Whenever bombers droned overhead, panic seized me. One day, while I was attending a prayer meeting held by a group of refugee women, an explosion sounded dangerously close. I bolted from my seat. *I must get to my children.* But the door was blocked by a woman whose head was bowed in prayer. I looked around the room. *Every* head was bowed in prayer. There was Anna Harder in the last stages of pregnancy; beside her sat Sarah Harder whose husband, Peter, was also at the Russian front. Like mine, their children were endangered by the air raid. Still, both women's heads were bowed in prayer. I slumped back into my chair wishing I could have faith like them. Yes, I said I trusted God to look after us, but these women actually expected Him to do it—even in an air raid. All I could think about was *I want to go home. Make it short. Say amen already.*

The weather turned very cold and stormy. One night, before going to bed, I closed the damper on the coal heater so that the house would stay warm all night. A couple of hours later, I woke up with a raging headache and an upset stomach. I slid out of bed, but my legs wouldn't support me and I fell to the floor. The whole room spun around me. *Carbon monoxide poisoning! I must get to the door.* But when I raised myself up, I fell back down again. Just then I heard Agnes calling, "Mommy, I feel sick." *I have to get to the door.* Holding onto the legs of furniture, I pulled myself forward. When I reached the door, I grabbed the door handle, and, using all my strength, I pushed the door open. A rush of cold, fresh air greeted me. I lay across the doorstep and vomited. For the rest of the night, I left the door open. Meanwhile I lay on the veranda, too weak to move, my head throbbing in pain.

In the morning, I checked on the children. Both Lena and Agnes felt ill, but Fred and Katie were fine. Since their bed was near a window, they must have had enough oxygen. Had I stayed asleep, we would have died. God in His mercy had awakened me. Truly our lives were in His hands.

One day I noticed lice crawling in my children's hair. From then on, every evening before bedtime, I opened their long braids and searched for lice. Since I had no fine-toothed comb, I parted their thick hair with my fingers strand by strand. Soon I felt lice crawling on my head. "Girls, please search my hair," I begged. But the girls weren't able to find the lice and remove them.

Yet my head itched and the crawling sensation kept me awake at night. *Why don't you pray for a comb?* Immediately I felt ashamed. *At this very moment thousands of brave young men, wounded in battle, are calling upon God, and you ask for a comb? God has better things to do than worry about the lice on your head.* So I refused to bother God with such a petty request.

The next morning I answered a knock on the door. A neighbour, whom I hardly knew, had come to call. "My husband arrived last night from Italy and he has brought me two fine-toothed combs," she said. " Last night, I couldn't sleep. All night long I felt a strong urging, like somebody was telling me, 'Why don't you bring Neta a comb?' So here's the comb." Looking rather embarrassed, she added, "I have no idea if you even need a comb."

"I do, I do!" I responded enthusiastically. "Thank you very much."

I could hardly believe it. Despite my lack of faith, God had taken note of my special need. He did care about the lice on my head. I realized then that nothing is too small for God if it concerns the welfare of His beloved children. We need never be ashamed to tell God everything that is in our hearts.

Christmas Eve 1944

On Christmas Eve the children and I were invited to a party two refuge women had made in another village five kilometres away. There was a lot of partisan activity (underground resistance) in the area going on, and it wasn't safe to be walking at night. Rumours had it that refugee women were being raped and their children molested. Still, I decided that the children deserved a little Christmas cheer. We would go.

"Tonight we're going to a party," I told them.

Seeing their excitement, I knew I was making the right decision. After supper, I dressed the younger children against the winter's cold. My two oldest didn't need any prompting. I put on my heavy winter coat, tied a kerchief around my head, and slipped on some warm felt boots. With one small breath, I blew out the small flame from an oil wick standing on the kitchen table. It was pitch dark now.

I opened the door and stepped onto the crisp snow covering the farmyard. A bright crescent moon hung above the Kerns' dark house. Because of the front being so close, all windows were heavily draped and the village lay in darkness. I lifted Katie to my back and took Fred's little hand. Lena and Agnes followed.

"Hang tight onto my collar," I instructed Katie.

When we reached the road, I hesitated for a brief moment. It would be too dangerous to take the road. You never knew who you'd run into. "We'll cut across the fields," I said.

The snow crunched as four pairs of feet punched holes in the white expanse of open fields. Above us, bright stars pierced the vault of sky and snow glistened on the trees. My arms began to ache so I put Katie down on the ground for a short rest. "Girls, recite your Christmas poems," I said. Their recitations made little white puffs in the cold night air. "When your turn comes, speak up loud and clear," I admonished. "No mumbling."

After awhile, I lifted Katie onto my back again, and we continued our walk. In about an hour, we arrived at our friends' house, also veiled in darkness. Yet, when the door opened, the children and I gasped at the brightness of candlelight emanating from a small Christmas tree. It cast a soft glow on the happy faces of mothers and children sitting on the floor, many of whom I recognized. We took our places and participated in the program. Each child said a poem or a Scripture. Then Weihnachtsmann entered the room, and gave each child a colourful ball made from scrunched up rags wrapped in rainbow coloured threads of wool. I smiled at our hostesses; they'd been busy unravelling old sweaters in order to make this wonderful surprise for our children. We concluded the program by singing our favourite Christmas carols: *"Stille Nacht, heilige Nacht"* (Silent Night, Holy Night) and *"Welch ein Jubel, welche Freude"* (What Rejoicing Comes at Christmas Time). Some mothers sang soprano, I joined the altos. *How strange to be singing about peace and joy at a time like this,* I thought. *But isn't that the message of Christmas? Jesus, the Light of the world, has come and no amount of darkness—even in this war-torn place—can put it out?* How I would need this truth in the coming days!

A Vision

Every day the Russian front came closer. I was terrified of the bombing, but even more of being captured by the Russians. At night I lay awake worrying: *Winter is a bad time to evacuate. Who will help us?* One night, after endlessly deliberating about what was to become of us, I fell into a fitful sleep. I dreamt I was climbing a steep hill. I carried Katie in my arms; the other children clutched my skirt from behind. It was night. Snow swirled around us. I saw a wagon trek going over a hill and into a valley; for miles and miles, a long line of refugees, some in wagons and some on foot. I heard drivers shout at their horses and, behind them, I saw women and children crammed into the wagons. The horizon was lit with the flickering of fires at the front. I hurried to the road.

"Please take us along," I called.

The wagons rumbled past me. Nobody stopped.

I called louder. But the desolate faces on the wagons looked past me as though they couldn't see or hear me. "Please," I shouted, "don't leave us here."

But the pounding of horses' hoofs and the scraping of wagon wheels on icy snow drowned out my cries. Then I heard a voice call out, "Neta, look up." I did. The black sky parted and a shaft of light, like a warm mantle, fell upon me and my children. Its warmth penetrated my whole body and a deep calm replaced the earlier panic. "The children and I are standing in His light," I mused.

Then I awoke.

For a few minutes I lay awake wondering at this dream, then I fell asleep again. Once more I was struggling up a hill with my children in tow. Wagons crammed with refugees rumbled past me on a frozen highway. But this time I saw a house at the top of the hill and from the gable two flags were suspended from a pole: the German flag with its swastika hung like a limp rag while the other flag, which I did not recognize, fanned out in a triumphant manner. I woke up confused and worried. Was this also a message from God? But it was unthinkable that the Germans would lose the war. Yes, we were fleeing, at the moment, but victory was sure to come. It was just a matter of time.

Evacuation Orders

On January 18, 1945, I sent Lena and Agnes to school but an hour later they returned.

"There's no school today," Lena said. I hurried to the shop to buy bread, but the shop was closed. What was going on?

Later that afternoon, the Germans issued an evacuation order. Unlike the time when we left Ukraine, there would be no transport provided. Every jeep and every train was needed for the military. We had to get away the best way we could. Those who had horses and wagons quickly got them ready. But what was I going to do? I had no wagon and no horses, and four children.

The Polish man whose house we had used the past few months said to me, "Neta, don't leave. Think of your children fleeing in this cold weather. Nothing will happen to you when the Russians come. Now the Kerns—they have to leave. Being Germans and despised estate owners, you know what will happen to them." He pointed his index finger to his head. "But, you'll be okay."

I thanked him for his kind words but told him I, too, wanted to leave. But how? How far would we get on foot? If the Russians didn't overtake us first, we'd surely freeze to death. Moments later Frau Kern dashed across the yard. "Neta, you want to go?"

"Yes," I cried.

"Then pack quickly. We're leaving in an hour." Once more, I stuffed our bedding and clothing into sacks, also a few tin cups and plates, and some food. I had only half a loaf of bread and some dried beans for the journey.

Suddenly, my Polish friend darkened the doorway. "You're leaving?"

I nodded my head.

"In that case, give me your husband's shoes," she said. "My husband's shoes are torn, and your husband won't need his."

I grabbed the shoes, hesitated a moment, then dropped them into the sack. *Give away Isaac's shoes? Wasn't that the same as giving up hope?* No, I wouldn't do that. "Sorry, my husband will need them when he comes home," I said. My friend shook her head, wished me good luck, then walked briskly across the yard.

CHAPTER TEN

Fleeing for our Lives

I T WAS DARK when the Kern's hay wagon stopped at the
front door. Kern handed the reins to Herta, his teenage
daughter, then hopped down to help me with the children
and my luggage. When I handed him my small singer sewing
machine, he said, "Leave that behind." But I insisted it must
come along. "It will be useful some day," I said. I didn't tell
him of the precious papers it held inside its case.

Kern flicked the reins and the horses began to move
out of the yard and into the street choked with wagons and
people trying to get away on foot. Suddenly a man jumped
in front of our horses and shouted, "For God's sake, take
this woman and her children along." A heavy coughing fit
racked his body and he couldn't say anymore. Franz Harder!
How could a man in the last stages of tuberculosis survive
this? And Anna, not fully recovered from giving birth, how
would she cope with four children, the youngest just two
weeks old? As I looked down, though, I saw Sarah Harder,
not Anna, standing beside the road with her seven children

looking frightened and forlorn, their few belongings lying in the snow.

"Those are my friends," I said to Kern. "Could you–?"

"Impossible," he said. "We can't strain the horses."

On the highway, tanks and jeeps thundered east. A wagon trek filled with refugees rumbled west. Gusts of wind blew snow into our faces and I covered the children with Isaac's heavy fur coat. Near the top of a hill, the horses skidded on the icy road. Drivers shouted at their horses and tried hard to keep their wagons on the road. Then the trek began to move again slowly over the hill and down into a valley. For miles and miles–a long line of refugees, some on wagons and some on foot. *I've seen this before,* I realized with a start. *My dream. Yes, it looked exactly like this.* I gazed up at the sky fully expecting the light to shine down upon us, but the sky remained black. Yet a deep peace filled me. In my mind's eye, I could see the light of God encircling us, as I'd seen it in the dream. It was God's message to me that, no matter what lay ahead, He would protect us.

The days and nights dragged on, and even though we made very few stops, we made slow progress. Sometimes a horse collapsed from the heavy strain of pulling too much weight. Then the horse and wagon were pushed into the ditch so the wagon trek could move on, leaving women and children standing beside their abandoned wagons. To lighten the load, people began to throw luggage overboard and soon the roadside was littered like a tornado had swept through the land. The cold wind blew relentlessly. My children's faces peeled and their lips cracked. The bread I had brought was frozen hard. Before I could break off a piece and give it to the children, I would hold it between my legs to thaw out. To stave off hunger, I gave each child a few beans to chew on. But what was I to do about their thirst? I strained my eyes looking for a Red Cross jeep beside the road where a cup of hot coffee or milk would be given and maybe a bowl of soup, but sometimes a whole day went by before we saw one. Going to the toilet was also a problem. At first my girls didn't want to use the potty pail in the wagon, but soon they had no choice. I would dump the contents overboard staining the snow. And still the trek moved on.

Most of the time, I walked beside the wagon. I stayed close because Katie started screaming as soon as she couldn't see me. When we entered a village, I left the wagon to beg for food for my children. Meanwhile the wagons kept moving. Usually people were kind and gave me something, but sometimes, I had to wander away quite a distance. When I got some food, I hurried back to the wagon–or where I thought it should be–but I couldn't always find it right away. In a panic, I ran along the wagon trek until I found our wagon. Relief washed over me when I saw the familiar faces of my children again. It was easy to get separated from one's children in this way, and I prayed fervently this would never happen to me.

We travelled in this caravan for three months. Driven on by the encroaching front, at first we dared not stop. But once the immediate danger passed, we slowed down our pace to spare the horses. We stopped at night to sleep in a barn on hay or in an evacuated house. Meanwhile, the horses got a good rest and a good feed. The houses were often fully furnished and the cupboards stocked with groceries–once I saw bread dough rising in a mixing bowl and laundry soaking in a tub. Obviously, the people had left in a great hurry. I always felt as though I was trespassing, walking into somebody else's house and using their amenities. I would take some groceries and use their beds, but I never felt free to help myself to clothes or other personal effects. Just once, though, I took a pair of men's shoes because mine were torn and my feet were often wet.

One day, on a side road, we met some good friends of the Kerns from Dieterwald. The Dittmans had two wagons: one for themselves and their two teenage girls, and one for a Polish man and his family. The families agreed to travel together.

In one abandoned village, we stayed for several days so that the horses could get a good rest. Wanting to somehow pay for our lodging, I joined some Polish women who were culling potatoes in a barn. One afternoon Lena came looking for me. As she was crossing the yard, a German shepherd attacked her: he threw her to the ground and bit her. Hearing her screams, I ran towards her, just as a man appeared and called off the dog. Thankfully, Lena was not hurt—the dog had bit into her overstuffed coat pocket, merely grazing the skin on her abdomen. But the following day, Lena received a greater shock. As she entered the yard, she saw the dog tied up near the barn. A man aimed a gun at him and fired. The dog yelped and blood spurted from his left shoulder. Another shot rang out, and the dog crumpled to the ground. Lena came running towards me.

"It's all my fault," she cried bitterly.

Sobs racked her body and her words came out in wounded pieces: "He killed...the dog...because of me."

"Shhh. Stop, Lena," I said. "He didn't kill him because he attacked you yesterday."

She looked at me with tear-filled eyes. "Like us, the man will soon be on the road and he can't take his dog along," I explained. "That's why he shot him." But I worried about my sensitive child. Hadn't Lena, who was such an ardent animal lover, seen enough suffering already?

Tired Of Running Away

One day several weeks into our flight, we entered Klemmerwitz, a small village near the city of Liegnitz on the Kaczawa River, in southwestern Poland. Except for a few Polish people, the houses were empty. We picked a comfortable house to spend the night in and went to bed.

The following morning as we gathered in the kitchen, Frau Dittman said, "I'm tired of running like a criminal. I vote we stay here."

Frau Kern nodded.

"We haven't hurt the Russians. Why would they want to hurt us?" Frau Dittman continued. My heart began to pound wildly and I felt the colour in my cheeks rising. Had we come this far only to surrender to the Russians? "That has nothing to do with it," I said. "They will view us as enemies simply because we're German-speaking." A heated discussion followed.

"Please listen to me," I begged. "The communists will take away your horses. Your husbands will be imprisoned and sent to Siberia. And our children will be sent to a state-run communist orphanage." My voice broke and I burst into tears. In the end, my protests did no good.

"Our horses are exhausted," Herr Kern said, "and we're running out of fodder." He looked at his wife and daughter for approval. "We will stay."

All the next day, I watched as wagons rumbled through the village in their flight from machine gun fire. Jeeps with wounded soldiers also passed through quickly. The shooting was so close now, that the windows and doors rattled. Mortar shells burst into the yard. Explosions filled the air with smoke and debris. Some houses went up in flames. The soldiers milling about the street looked dirty and dishevelled. In the back of one army truck, I saw a pile of dead bodies.

At night as I lay awake in my bed, I felt numb. *Well, this is it,* I thought. *The front is here. I hope the end is quick.* Suddenly, Frau Dittman bolted out of bed. "I can't stand this anymore," she yelled. "Let's go."

In a flash, everyone was out of bed and throwing stuff back onto the wagons. The men hitched the horses and we clambered aboard. The noise of the shooting spooked the horses and they flew down the streets. At one checkpoint, a soldier shouted at us, "Crazy people! Why did you wait so long?" All night and the next day we raced west, dodging army trucks and barricades. We didn't dare stop.

The following evening, the men decided it was safe enough to stop for the night. We arrived at a large barn, but the door was locked. Above the door, in the servant's quarters, a light was shining. Kern pounded on the stable door and shouted for help. A small curtain parted a little; a woman looked down at us; then she dropped the curtain, and the light went out. Nobody came to open the door. I was angry enough that if I had had a stone in my hand, I would have thrown it through the window. My children had been crammed into this cold wagon for twenty hours without food or water. How could people be so callous?

Meanwhile, Kern and Dittman kicked in the barn door. They tossed some hay onto the floor and we bedded down. Soon my children and I were fast asleep. Moments later, a loud noise woke me. I saw a horse rear and kick at a stall. I jumped up and looked about me. *Where am I? How did I get here?* I couldn't remember. Terrified, I ran up and down the barn. I stumbled past some people sleeping on the hay. *Who are they and why are they here?* I peered into the faces, but I couldn't recognize anyone. A man raised himself up on one elbow. "What do you want, Neta?" he asked.

"Who are you?" I asked.

"I'm Kern."

"I don't know you."

"Neta, we've travelled together for two months..."

"But I don't know you."

Kern took my hand and led me to my sleeping children. "Do you know who they are?"

"My children," I choked. "How did they get here?"

As I listened to my friend explain, I tried so hard to remember, but I couldn't. My mind was blank, frozen in fear. Suddenly, a horse reared again and gave a loud snort. A woman jumped to her feet and yelled, "Shut up." Like a flash, I recognized Frau Dittman. A torrent of memories cascaded into my tired brain and brought me back to reality. "Thank God," I cried. He had brought me back from the brink of insanity, a terror worse than death.

The next morning, a well-dressed man came into the barn. "Please, forgive what happened last night," he said. "My men were simply obeying orders. I had no idea there were women and children." He cleared his throat awkwardly. "Would you please come into the house for breakfast." We followed him into a large house. After a good meal, we rested awhile before resuming our trek west.

Will We Always Live On A Wagon?

Just as the sun was sinking and the evening chill settled, we entered another town square. It was a cauldron of shouting, moving humanity. Our men unhitched the wagon and told the women to find a place to spend the night. I climbed off the wagon and stood undecided. I dreaded walking from house to house and begging for shelter, only to have the doors slammed in my face. Suddenly, I felt a tug. I looked down at a small girl who had taken my hand.

"Do you need lodging for the night?" she asked.

"Yes."

"Come with me then," she smiled. "My mother sent me to invite someone home for the night."

I blinked. Was I seeing an angel? No, before me stood a girl with bright blue eyes and blond braids wearing a navy blue coat with a hood; she looked to be about six or seven, the same age as my Agnes. Her round face radiated a welcome. She led the way to a small house not far from the town square. At the door, a woman greeted us kindly and asked us to come in. Soon she placed a hot meal on the table and invited us to sit down and eat. At bedtime, she took me into the master bedroom and told me the children and I would be sleeping in the big bed with the eider down.

"No. No. We'll sleep on the floor," I said.

But she insisted. "We will be in your situation soon," she sighed. "I hope someone will help us out then."

After one night in this gracious home, we went back to the wagon. My children got so tired of sitting, day after day, in a cramped position on an open wagon. It was so cold; I'm sure we would have frozen to death had it not been for Isaac's thick fur coat. Sometimes four-year old Fred would look longingly at a house with smoke curling from a chimney and ask, "Can we live there?"

"No, somebody else lives there."

"Mama, where do we live then?"

"On this wagon."

"Will we always live on a wagon?" His plaintive voice tore at my heart, yet, we were fortunate. Many people were fleeing on foot with whatever they could carry or pull in a small wagon.

At the end of February, the weather was still very cold. We slept in our clothes for several weeks in a row. How I longed for a hot bath and a clean change of clothes. Once more we were infested with lice, and the itching was almost unbearable. Luckily, I still had the comb given me by my kind neighbour in Poland. One day, among a group of refugees, I met her again. What a terrible story she told me! As she was fleeing, *both* of her twins had frozen to death, but there had been no time to bury her children. She left their stiff, little bodies lying beside the road, hoping some kind farmer would bury them.

You're On Your Own!

In Vogelsdorf, 23 kilometres east of Berlin, Kern stopped his wagon in a busy town square teeming with soldiers and refugees.

"Frau Loewen," he said awkwardly, "our horses are sick. This is as far as I can take you." Quickly he unloaded our baggage. I turned to Frau Kern and hugged her.

"Thank you," I said. "You've been very kind to take us this far."

As I watched them leave, a feeling of desolation over-whelmed me. What was I to do? I sat down on a sack and took two-year-old Katie onto my lap. The children huddled close to me and still we shivered in the chill of mid-March. Then I stood up, put Katie down, and said to the children, "Wait here for me. I'll find us a place for the night."

Leaving nine-year-old Lena in charge, I walked into town. I stopped at the first house and knocked. "Do you have lodging for me and my family?" The answer was no. I walked from house to house asking the same question. Sometimes a slight hesitation made me hopeful, but when I mentioned I had four children, the people quickly said no, they had no room. Door after door closed in my face. It was dusk when I returned to my children, all of them crying from hunger and cold. I stared at their frostbitten cheeks

135

and their cracked lips. There was no place for them to warm up and I couldn't even give them any food. Bone-weary, I dropped to the frozen ground and covered my head. *Our situation is hopeless*, I thought. *I want to die.*

Somebody grabbed my arm and shook me. "Woman, get up! Can't you hear your children crying?" I opened my eyes and saw a German soldier leaning over me.

"I've watched your children all afternoon," he stormed. "What's going on?"

"I've gone from house to house and nobody will take us in," I said weakly.

"We'll see about that!" he said gruffly. "Come with me."

I stumbled to my feet. The soldier picked up Katie and cradled her in one arm. With the other hand, he took Fred's hand. "Let's go," he said. I didn't have time to collect our things, so I left them in the square. The girls and I hurried to keep up with his determined strides. At a house not far from the town square, he pounded on the front door. A woman opened the door a crack, her face registering irritation.

"Give this woman and her children a hot meal and a warm place to sleep," the soldier said.

"My God!" the woman exclaimed. "I have no room."

"Find room," the soldier commanded.

"But my house is full—"

"*Donnerwetter,*" the soldier shouted, "open this door or I'll shoot you."

"Come in," she said grudgingly. "But I don't know where I'll put you."

"I'll be back in the morning," the soldier said. "Take good care of them." He looked menacingly at the woman to drive home the point that he meant business. Then he turned and left.

Our appointed hostess gave us a hot meal, then she provided blankets and told us to find a place to sleep on the floor in the kitchen. Her house was indeed full of soldiers. The following morning, she served us breakfast. About mid-morning, true to his word, our Good Samaritan-soldier returned, pulling a small wagon with all our belongings in it. He had retrieved them from the town square. He placed Katie and Fred in the wagon on top of our stuff.

"Now come along," he said. "We'll find you another place." He pulled the wagon while the rest of us followed behind. In about an hour, we arrived in Landeshut, a transition refugee camp.

"You can't stay more than a few days here," the soldier said. "But by then something else will turn up." He tipped his hat, and said, "*Auf wiedersehen. Und Gott befohlen.*" (God be with you); then he walked briskly away.

More Angels Of Mercy

On the third day at the camp I was told, "Your time is up. This is the last meal you will receive here." A bus had come to transport us to another refugee camp, but to go there, we would have to leave our luggage behind. As I watched one family auctioning off their clothes and bedding, I shivered in my threadbare sweater. *I can't part with our blankets and Isaac's fur coat,* I thought. *The children will freeze to death.* And yet, if I wanted to go on the bus, I would have to give up even that. As I stood there trying to decide what to do, the auctioneer held up a large blue sweater. "How much?" he asked. I made a low bid. His wife, a large woman with a cigarette dangling from her mouth, grabbed the sweater and tossed it in my direction. "Here, you take it," she said sizing me up. "Nobody needs it more!" I wore the sweater for many years and this random act of kindness warmed me each time.

I'm not sure why I decided against going on the bus for I had no other place to go. Something (God, perhaps) stopped me and drew me back into Vogelsdorf. I told my children to play quietly in a corner of a large room. (The refugee camp had been a linen factory before the war.) Then I went back into the village looking for another place for us. On the street, I met the woman we had stayed with three nights before. I was surprised when she greeted me cordially.

"We've been at the transition camp but we must move again," I told her.

"Where to?"she inquired.

"I have no idea."

She looked away thoughtfully, then her face brightened. "I know a place," she said. "Come, I'll show you." As we walked through the village she spoke of her friends, the Webers, good people, she said, who had suffered much in the war. They would surely find a room for us. At a tiny house, bordering on a small forest, she stopped.

"Here we are," she said, and left without making an introduction.

Timidly, I knocked. A woman, bent with age, opened the door. She listened carefully to my dilemma, then went back inside to confer with her husband. Soon she returned. "Julius and I want you to come," she said. "Bring your children. In the meantime, I shall get your room ready." What music to my ears! I hurried back to the refugee camp.

I'm not sure how I transported our baggage from the transition camp at Landeshut to the Weber's house in Vogelsdorf. (I still had my Singer sewing machine with its precious cargo.) But soon we were settled in a small room in the home of Julius and Anna Weber. There were two single beds, a table and two chairs, a wash stand, and a heater.

It was a small two-bedroom house with a barn attached to it. In the trees nearby, birds chirped merrily, welcoming spring. Warmer temperatures coaxed buds to swell. Every day more delicate greenery showed in the underbrush. On the sloping hillsides, three goats foraged for grass among melting snow patches. The Webers used a well at the bottom of a hill. When I saw old Anna Weber struggle up the hill with a pailful of water, I ran to help her. "Please, let me do this," I said. She readily agreed, and from then on, I hauled many buckets of water each day for her and her three goats. The children and I also collected firewood in the forest.

Soon after we arrived, I heated water for our baths. It had been three months since we'd had the chance to get clean. I borrowed a large tub from the Webers. First, the children had their baths, from the youngest to the oldest, just like we had done at home in Ukraine. Since I had no soap, I let each child soak extra long. Then I rubbed off the grime and dead skin. Of course, we had no shampoo, but Anna Weber gave me an egg which I beat up and used like shampoo. After the last child was bathed and tucked into bed, I added more hot water. Then I climbed into the tub and soaked. I closed my eyes and tried to absorb the pure comfort of it. How long I had waited for this! How good to wash away weeks of sweat and dirt! After my bath, I soaked our clothes in the same water. I would wash them tomorrow and hang them outside to dry in the sun.

Dressed in clean clothes and feeling human again, I trudged back into the village to register at the municipal hall, so I could get ration cards for my family.

"What's your name?" the clerk asked.

"Anganetha Loewen."

"*An-ga-ne-tha*," he drew out each syllable mockingly. "Where did your parents find that ugly name? It's worse than Constantinople."

I tried to dismiss his rude comment, but he wouldn't let it be. "Anganetha give yourself a different name–a good German name," he said.

"Like what?" I asked.

"Anneliese, Adelheid, Agnes..." he shrugged. " I don't care. Just choose something other than *An-ga-ne-tha*." He rolled his eyes.

"Write Agnes," I said.

The clerk's attitude didn't really surprise me. When the Germans occupied our village in Ukraine they had insisted that men with old- fashioned Jewish names take on modern German names. So, my husband Isaac became Fritz. My nephew David became Victor. A friend named Abraham became Franz. But it seemed that some *Reichsdeutsche*, (citizens of Germany) like the clerk, were adverse to all old-fashioned names. Never mind, I liked the name Agnes too.

As the children and I collected dry pine cones and sticks for firewood and piled them up in the woodshed, the Webers sat on the veranda and watched us. I think it reminded them of happier times when their children were small and still at home with them.

"We had three sons," Anna said softly. "All of them were drafted into the German army. One is killed, one is missing, and one is fighting at the front." She dabbed her eyes with a hankie. "We keep hoping and praying–Julius and I–that God will hear us and bring them home again. Perhaps, if we help refugees here at home, God who sees all will help our sons far away. "

After milking the goats, Anna Weber would often bring me a small bucket of warm milk. "For the children," she'd smile. Then with a twinkle in her blue eyes she'd add, "Don't let Father know." Sometimes Julius Weber would open my door a crack and shove in a small basket of potatoes or eggs. "For you," he'd whisper; "Don't let Mother know." They were good people.

Even though the Webers said my children and I could stay with them until the war ended, I felt we needed to move on. One day, two weeks after we had arrived at the Webers, I heard of a train headed west which would take only old people and women with small children. I registered for it. By now, I'd lost track of all my people from Ukraine, but I hoped to find them further west.

On The Road Again

On Easter Sunday morning, 1945, a man came with a wagon to take us to the train station where he helped unload our baggage. "That's all," he said, as he hopped back onto the wagon and prepared to leave. Quickly, I made a mental check—Isaac's big fur coat was missing.

"Sir, you forgot the fur coat, " I called.

But he seemed not to hear me. He flicked the reins and the horses trotted off. *Never mind, it's spring,* I said to myself. *Thank God we had the fur coat in winter when we needed it.* It would have been too heavy to lug around anyway.

The train began to move slowly. I didn't know where we were going, and I didn't care as long as we escaped the terrible fighting. But even that was doubtful, for often the train would stop because an air strike up ahead had destroyed the rails or a bridge had been blown up, and repairs needed to be made. I felt like we were a sitting target, trapped in an idle train, while bombs fell either in front or behind us.

With the train so overcrowded, there were only two seats for our family of five. For a while, I sat down holding Katie on my lap with Fred and one of the girls sitting beside me. Lena and Agnes took turns standing in the aisle. Then I stood and all four children squeezed into the two seats. Once a day we received something to eat. Across the aisle from us sat two old women who complained that they couldn't sleep at night because my girls were lying on their feet. To prevent this from happening again, I forced myself to stay awake for two nights, but the third night, I couldn't stay awake anymore. I simply fell over. As long as I live, I'll give God thanks for a place to lie down at night, even if it's just on a pile of straw in a barn.

Our train snaked into Regensburg the morning after an air strike had destroyed the city. Nothing but a smouldering heap of ruins remained. The train station was also hit and the tracks were demolished. I could see crews of men and women working up ahead, extinguishing fires and clearing rubble off the train tracks. They worked feverishly for one whole day and one whole night before the train moved again. As I watched their dedicated efforts, I felt very grateful to them, but I also felt angry at the destruction created by war.

CHAPTER ELEVEN

Eggerding, Northern Austria (1945-1947)

THE TRAIN ENTERED northern Austria and stopped in a small depot called Andorf where we disembarked. I told the children to sit on our luggage while I went inside to enquire as to what we should do next. "Before nightfall, you will be picked up by an Austrian farmer," I was told. Soon the farmers came with their wagons and scanned the platform filled with refugees. I felt like we were slaves on an auction block. Since the farmers wanted field hands, nobody gave us a second look. Gradually the crowd on the platform thinned and only a few refugees remained. Toward evening, there were only six of us left: an old woman with a grossly swollen leg who could hardly walk and me and my four children. I could understand why we hadn't been chosen. A frail-looking woman with four children, the oldest nine and the youngest two, was clearly not a good bargain.

Before locking up, the station master made a phone call on our behalf. In the growing darkness, I heard another wagon rumble into the station. A man hopped down and told me and my children to get on. He loaded our luggage, then helped the old woman into a seat beside him. As we left Andorf, only a few stars pierced the sky above us. We left the town, crossed rolling farmlands, and skirted a small forest. Then we entered a village and stopped at a school building converted into a refugee camp.

The driver helped me carry our luggage into a crowded classroom. All along the walls, on piles of straw covered with army blankets, people were already sleeping. Seeing us enter, an old woman moved over and made room for us in one corner of the classroom. I spread a blanket over the exposed straw and told my children to lie down and go to sleep. Just as I was about to fall asleep, I sensed a familiar crawling on my head and over my whole body. Oh, no, lice again!

The following day, we were served a bowl of oatmeal porridge for breakfast. This became our daily fare, except on Sunday, when a stewed prune crowned the oatmeal porridge. Eggerding was a small village nestled at the foot of a large Roman Catholic Church. On the steeple was a clock which chimed every hour. There was a bakery, a grocery shop, and a small hotel. The village was surrounded by rolling hills dotted with farms. Fields of newly-sprouting wheat or rye formed soft-green patches among the darker green of pasture lands. Across the church was a large cemetery ringed by tall poplar trees. Not far from the refugee camp, was a small forest which became our sanctuary. There my children and I found some peace and quiet. The forest also became our private delousing spot. Trying to rid ourselves of lice became a daily ritual. I would ask the children to undress and sit down on a fallen log with just their panties on. Lena and Agnes had to search their own clothing. "Be sure to look in every seam, " I'd say. "Tell me when you see a louse." But all too quickly they'd announce, "I'm finished. May I get dressed now?" The children were more interested in finding pine cones and other treasures of the forest to play with.

"First, your hair," I'd say. "Open your braids."

Reluctantly, they obeyed, but in their eyes I read, *Mom, what's so important about a louse?* Well, I had declared war on lice, and I wasn't about to be deterred. After doing Lena's long, blond hair, I investigated Agnes' auburn hair, taking it apart strand by strand. I felt a moment of triumph each time I squished a louse between my nails.

"Now search my hair," I'd say. But my girls never found a louse even though I knew they were there. Meanwhile, the old woman sleeping beside me was a veritable nursery of lice. I could see them crawling all over her grey hair and tattered clothing. She merely flicked them off.

One morning, the bürgermeister of Eggerding came to tell us that the school was needed for military personnel and we would have to evacuate. In the afternoon, an army truck took us to the city of Schärding, but every refugee camp was full to overflowing. By evening, we still hadn't found a place to stay. "I'll just take you back where you came from," our driver said. The night was dark and warm. We entered a small forest that twinkled with little lights which looked like bits of fire that blinked on and off among the blackened trees. "What's that?" I asked a woman huddled beside me at the back of the truck.

"Fire flies."

"How beautiful!" I exclaimed.

She looked at me crossly. "We have no place to go; what's so beautiful about that?"

"Fire flies are beautiful," I said quietly. It might seem crazy to find comfort in fire flies when we were homeless once again, but I figured that God had sent them to cheer up our dreary night.

The lights were out when we arrived back at the school and the door was locked. I'm not sure where we slept that night, probably on the back of the truck parked in front of the school. The following morning we watched three hundred Austrian boy-soldiers prepare to leave for the front. Man-sized uniforms hung loosely from their narrow shoulders and their faces peering out from underneath army caps looked so young. *Some boys haven't even had a voice change,* I thought. *Now they're given guns and told to fight.* As the trucks roared off down the street towards the combat zone, I wanted to cry. How many of those boys would return to their families alive?

With the soldiers gone, we moved off the truck and back into the classroom. But most refugees who had left the day before did not return. They must have found lodging elsewhere.

The following day, a group of 120 orphan children with four teachers arrived. An elderly couple, Herr and Frau Dührer, were the house parents. They assigned the boys to one classroom and the girls to another. My children and I stayed in a corner in the girls' classroom near the outside door. But before everyone settled down, the old straw was taken out, the floor was mopped with disinfectant, and fresh straw was piled against the walls. *No more lice,* I thought. But my joy was short-lived for these orphan children had lice too and they also had scabies. Soon the telltale itchy rash appeared between our fingers. To get away from the noise of the children, we spent every possible moment outside. We roamed across the meadows dotted with buttercups, clover, daisies, and Hansel and Gretel flowers, so named because pink and blue flowers grow on the same stem. But our favourite spot was the small forest. I loved watching the children in their creative play. A hollow tree trunk became their play house carpeted with moss and outfitted with twig-furniture made by tying sticks together with vines. Pine cones became their dolls: two large cones represented mother and father, smaller cones, the children. Lena dug up buttercups growing beside a small stream and transplanted them in a little garden plot she had prepared by the front door. Agnes and Fred gathered pebbles and made a path through the garden. We stayed in this peaceful atmosphere until supper time, then returned to the refugee camp.

We bought our food with ration cards, but it was never enough. We could eat in one day what was supposed to last for one week. At the refugee camp the only food we received was our morning bowl of porridge. For a Sunday treat a stewed prune lay on top of the porridge. I smiled at little Katie as she ate tiny circles of porridge around the prune, leaving this treat to the last. Then she'd pop the prune into her mouth and savour it for a few minutes before swallowing it. For lunch I served a cup of milk and a small piece of bread. Supper, at five, was a small helping of cooked beans. (I still had some beans I brought from our home in Ukraine.)

In time, the children suffered from malnutrition. They became listless and lost interest in play. Fred would sit on the yard and stare at the huge clock on the church steeple. He had asked me so often "Is it time to eat yet?" that I had taught him the position of the arms of the clock at 5 p.m. One day Fred asked me, "Is there lots of food in heaven?"

"We won't need any food in heaven," I said, surprised by the question. "Because we won't be hungry."

"I'll be hungry," he said, "and if there's no food in heaven, I don't want to go there."

To supplement their meagre rations, refugees swarmed to the farmers to ask for food. We called it hamstering, not begging, for we offered our services in payment. (The word "hamstering" comes from the industrious little animal which carries grain in its large cheek pouches.) I would take either Lena or Agnes with me. We'd leave the village and hike up country roads to farm buildings that resembled a square. The owner's home, the boarding house for the labourers, and the barns all faced a court yard in the middle. Often the back of the barn with its manure pile was facing the road. I found this most peculiar. Timidly I would knock on a door–hoping it was the right one–and prepare to say my speech. Sometimes I'd receive a few potatoes, carrots, or a beet to take home.

One day, as I knocked on the door of a large farmhouse, I heard a clomping of wooden shoes, and moments later, a rotund woman opened the door. "If you could spare a few potatoes," I began. "I'll gladly do some work—"

"No potatoes," the woman said and slammed the door shut.

As Lena and I crossed the farmyard, we passed a large barn, and not far from the open door lay an enormous pile of potatoes. Lena's blue eyes lit up in disbelief as she scanned the pile, then they clouded over. "Doesn't she know lying is a sin?" she asked. Another afternoon, after walking many kilometres all Agnes and I garnered was one egg, but we picked some wild raspberries on the way home, and for supper we ate fresh raspberries topped with a beaten egg.

My daily ration of food included one litre of milk which I fetched from the village shoemaker. After his wife milked their three goats in the evening, I would arrive with a small pail and she would fill it with warm milk. But soon the milk lost its golden lustre. It became translucent and when I cooked it, it curdled. *Something's wrong with this milk,* I thought. The next day, the same thing happened. This went on for several days. One day, I determined to find out why. I arrived at the kitchen door just as the shoemaker's wife came from the barn, a bucket of rich, frothy milk in her hand. She grabbed my container and went inside, asking me to wait outside. But quietly, I followed her into the kitchen. I saw how she pretended to wash out my pail but she didn't dump the water. She diluted the milk with the water in the pail.

"I have enough water at home," I said.

She was so startled that she dropped my pail. Milk splashed onto her feet and ran across the kitchen floor.

She whirled around, her face flaming red, " Damn you, refugee!" she yelled, "Go back to Russia where you belong." I picked up my container and headed for the door. "Just wait, the Americans are coming and they'll drive you home,"she shouted in parting.

As I trudged home without milk that evening, bitter thoughts boiled within my heart, and I wished all kinds of evil upon her: *Let her husband be missing; let her children go hungry; let her be destitute in a foreign country.* Tears blurred the path. Suddenly, a friendly voice startled me. "Good evening, Madam." I looked up to see a nun's smiling face. "Could you please tell me where the vicar lives?" That's all she said, yet the kindness in her eyes and voice restored to me a sense of dignity. *The shoemaker's wife is to be pitied, not hated,* I thought.

I could forgive the shoemaker's wife because into my mind flashed a memory of a time when I had been the cause of a young person's grief. One day, I found a fine-toothed comb on the schoolyard. I knew it must belong to one of the orphan girls and I should return it, but I decided to keep it just for a few days. (I had lost my comb when I lent it to a woman on the trek.) *I will use it until my lice are gone and then I will return it,* I said to myself. Among the orphan girls was a sad, little girl who was frequently punished for wetting her pants. But it wasn't really her fault. Because she had scabies, her hands were bandaged so that she couldn't pull her panties down in time. I felt very sorry for her. One day, her long, blond curls were sheared and she hung her head in shame. At first, I felt outrage—how could they do this to her? Then I remembered a rule the house parents made with the orphan children: you lose your comb, you lose your hair. The comb I had found and kept must belong to her. My tardiness in returning it had brought upon her this added humiliation. Of course, I returned the comb, but it was too late. Trying to somehow make up for the grief I had caused, I brought the little girl food whenever I could spare some.

Across from the schoolyard stood a stone house with a barn attached to one end. Often I saw a young woman working in the yard or driving cows from the barn after milking. In time, Resl and I became friends. Resl worked for Mühlböcks, who owned the rooming house and also the grocery store in the village. One day I told her about what happened at the shoemaker's. "I'm not surprised," she said. "She's a bad-tempered woman."

"But now I have no milk."

"Why don't you go to Bramberger's. They'll give you some."

Brambergers were the rich people in town who owned a hotel, a butchery, a hog and dairy farm, and much land surrounding the village. Frau Bramberger readily agreed to give me one litre of milk each day.

The Americans Are Coming!

On May 7, 1945, Germany surrendered to the Allies and the war ended. With great jubilation Austrian people hung white flags out of every window, and a funny assortment of white flags it was: pillow cases, towels, body shirts—whatever we could find that was white. The excitement in the village reached a fever pitch. There was great merriment in the streets. I stood by the window and pondered the strange events of my life brought about by this war. In three decades I had lived under the Russians, the Germans, and now the Americans. What would they be like? Would they send me back to Russia like the shoemaker's wife had said? I shuddered. They could shoot me, but I would not go back.

I glanced across the street and saw some refugees break down the door to Mühlböck's store and moments later carry out armfuls of groceries. I felt a twinge of sweet revenge. For weeks we had gone hungry while the Austrians had eaten plenty. Let them know what it feels like to be plundered. The thought, *Why not help yourself?* flashed through my mind. Yes, why not? My children could use some good food for a change. I left my place by the window and hurried towards the door. Suddenly, a voice arrested me: "Your heavenly Father knows that you have need of all these things." I stopped in my tracks. Would I resort to stealing or would I trust God to meet my need? "God help me," I whispered, "I want to trust You." I sat down on my bed of straw, determined not to give in to temptation.

An hour later, I heard the rumble of army jeeps. I jumped up and peeked out of the window. The Americans were coming! Soldiers in a strange uniform soon came into the school and looked intently at all the children sitting on their beds of straw. After a brief inspection tour, the soldiers left.

The Americans set up camp in the Brambergers' hotel. I found these strange, yet friendly soldiers, most intriguing. They lounged in their jeeps with their feet up on the dashboard. They called loudly across the street, "Hello, Mama." They threw candies to the children. They played a funny kind of game in the meadow hitting a ball with a long bat. And they were forever chewing. Whatever did they eat that needed so much chewing? (I'd never heard of chewing gum before!) What a group of relaxed and friendly men they were, not regimented like the German soldiers.

Soon after their arrival, the soldiers cleaned up the refugee camp. They removed the infested straw, and replaced it with fresh, clean straw. A medical clinic was set up. One day, each of us women and children lined up to have DDT powder sprinkled into our clothes and onto our hair. From that day, the crawling and itching stopped; the lice were gone. I felt human again.

One day, an American officer wanted to see me. *Oh, no, he's going to tell me we have to leave.* Instead, he spoke kindly to me and wanted to know how the orphans were being treated. Did the directors distribute the food fairly? "Yes," I said. "They don't have much, but whatever they have, they distribute fairly." His interest in the orphans astounded me. *The Americans treat refugees like valued human beings,* I thought. *Some Austrians may be disappointed by this.*

Soon plans were made to empty the entire refugee camp. Some of the orphan children with their houseparents moved into the Bramberger's hotel and others returned to their home in East Germany. My children and I were sent to a farm near Eggerding to find lodging. But when our wagon arrived at the gate, it was locked. A woman stuck her head out of a window and shouted, "My husband has gone to the field. You'll have to wait until he gets back."

It started to rain and we got drenched. "*Unsinn!*" (It's ridiculous!) the driver grumbled, "You can't just sit here and get soaked." He pounded on the door again, but no luck. The gate remained barred. Finally, the farmer arrived on horseback. He stared at us, disgust written all over his sunburnt face. "I ask Bramberger for field hands," he sneered, " and he sends me a kindergarten!" As he turned to go into the house, he yelled over his shoulder, "Tell Bramberger, I have my own kindergarten."

Hungry and shivering in our wet clothes, we arrived back in Eggerding at the small hotel. In one room the light was shining. I entered holding Katie in my arms and Fred by one hand. Agnes and Lena stood close behind. A small puddle formed on the floor where we were standing. A group of men were sitting around tables drinking cider with Bramberger presiding a meeting. He walked towards me and put his hand on my wet shoulder. "What's wrong, Frau Loewen?"

"The farmer doesn't want us."

"Doesn't want you!" Bramberger snapped. "Tomorrow I'll send a letter with you, and he'll want you all right."

"I'm not going back."

"Frau Loewen, what do I do with you then?" he asked.

"Send her back to the school building," a man volunteered.

Soon we were knocking on the custodian's door. Even though it was late and Fräulein Klaffenback had already gone to bed, she received us kindly. Quickly, she made a fire in the stove. "Hang your wet clothes on the backs of the chairs," she said, "here by the warm stove." Then she fixed us some beds on the floor. The next morning, warm sunshine spilled over the schoolyard. I spread our clothes on the grass and soon they were dry. With the custodian's permission, we moved into a room on the second floor. For the time being, we had a shelter and nobody bothered us.

Next door to the school building lived a family named Wiesmeier. Their two girls were the same age as my two. Our girls became good friends and often played together. I think a highlight of their day was a visit to the American camp, always at meal times. The girls would linger at the door, shyly holding a small pot in their hands hoping for leftovers. Seeing the longing in their eyes, many a soldier stopped eating. "Come here," he'd call and hand over half a can of peaches or sardines or spam, a chocolate bar, or a slice of bread. My girls returned home proudly displaying their bounty. "Girls, it's not polite to watch the soldiers eat," I'd say, but, in truth, I was grateful for the soldiers' generosity.

A Home At Last

One day at the end of July, the bürgermeister asked me to vacate the school, as it was needed for school children. He handed me a letter saying, "I have found a place for you at the Mühlböcks." My stomach lurched. I had met this elegant store owner a few times before and she had always been very aloof. She wouldn't want us! But what choice did I have? I delivered the letter to the maid at the door. She snatched it from my hand and slammed the door shut. Shaken, I returned to the bürgermeister and begged him to find us another place, but he spoke so kindly to me that I agreed to give it another try. The following day, a man came to tell me he had been sent by Frau Mühlböck to help us move into the rooming house where Resl lived.

We moved into a corner room on the ground floor to the right of the main entrance. Iron bars across the windows and a heavy iron door spoke of a time past when this room had been a secure storage place or perhaps a jail cell. Our room was furnished with two single beds, a table and chairs, a wash stand, and a wood stove. I scrubbed until everything was clean. Then I sewed little curtains for the windows, and spread a cloth over the table. Lena and I slept in one bed; the other three children shared the second bed. Fred slept with his head at the foot end. Sometimes his feet got tangled up with his sisters' feet and there was a brief skirmish, but most of the time, it worked just fine.

A long hallway led to a barn. To the right of the hall were four rooms: ours and three others occupied by field hands. A flight of stairs led to more rooms for rent at the front and a hayloft at the back. The Kallinger family, who had a boy Lena's age and a girl Agnes' age, occupied the suite to the right, and Frau Schmolz and Frau Marklin each had a room to the left. At the far end of the hayloft was a bathroom which all fourteen occupants of the house used. Since the hayloft was pitch-dark in the evening, and we had no flashlight, my girls waited as long as possible before going to the bathroom. They climbed the steps, pushed open a large door to the hayloft, then groped their way along a wall to a tiny cubicle at the far end that had a flush toilet. They flicked a switch and a single light bulb, dangling from the ceiling, sprang to life. When they had finished, they turned off the light, and groped their way back in the inky darkness. It happened on one occasion that, when the girls were halfway to the door, an eery sound came floating down from somewhere above them. *What's that?* The sound grew louder, came closer, and then took form. A ghost! White arms like giant bat wings undulated in slow motion reaching for them. The girls let out a blood curdling scream. The ghost burst into laughter and, with a thump, landed at their feet.

Before I could get to my girls, I heard a woman's loud voice calling, "Hansi, get in here! Quit scaring the girls!" His mother and I soon became good friends.

Running water for the whole house came from a tap in the barn. I could see how difficult it was for Frau Marklin, who was lame, to carry water up a long flight of stairs, so I offered to carry water to her room and to take the ashes from her stove downstairs. For this service, she gave me food on Fridays when she was fasting.

Since nobody seemed to be appointed to clean the hall, I began to sweep the floor every day, and on Saturdays, I scrubbed it. One day, Frau Mühlböck surveyed the clean hall, our freshly scrubbed room, and the tidy yard. "Thank God, you're here, Frau Loewen," she said. "Even the yard is swept." A few weeks later she said, "From now on you need not pay me rent." Of course, I was delighted. Then one day in fall, she offered, "You may go into the orchard and pick up all the windfalls." Since food was still very scarce, this was a great help.

Finding enough food to eat was a constant challenge. I worked at many odd jobs for which people paid me with food or money. I preferred food because money couldn't buy much. I cleaned houses and I scrubbed laundry on a scrub board, then carried it to the village pond for rinsing. (In the winter I had to chop a hole in the ice before I could dip the clothes into the frigid water–each piece three times. That was the Austrian way!) When there was a funeral, Wiesmeiers, who were care takers of the church and graveyard, sometimes asked me to help dig a grave. We used spades and worked quickly. Sometimes in digging up an old grave, we found black silk that wasn't rotten yet. Apparently, years ago, Austrian women were buried with a black silk veil. It always amazed me how well preserved the silk was so many years later. After the graveside service and the coffin was lowered, I helped them fill the grave and plant flowers on top. Frau Wiesmeier always gave me a good loaf of bread for doing the job.

I also mucked out pig barns—even though I was afraid of pigs. Early in the morning, before the children were awake, I went to feed the Bramberger's sixty pigs and clean the barn. Then I filled a huge cauldron with potatoes and boiled them for tomorrow's feeding. My boss allowed me to take home some cooked potatoes and this often became our supper.

After a quick breakfast of milk and bread with other field hands, I hurried home to wake up my children and give them their breakfast. "Mom, you stink," they'd tease and hold their noses. I would dress little Katie, encourage Fred to wash his face in the basin, plait the girls' hair and send them off to school. Then I'd hurry to the fields to work in haying or harvesting. It was a comfort to know that in my absence Lena and Agnes would be under the supervision of their teacher at school, but I worried about leaving little Katie and Fred by themselves. Granted, my good friends Frau Kallinger and Frau Wiesmeier were nearby and they assured me the children were always welcome to come to them, but as I feared, accidents did happen. One time little Katie fell into the village pond and, had it not been for Lena's loud yelling, which attracted a boy who plunged in and pulled her out, she would have drowned. Another time, Katie ran across the yard and fell, just as a motorbike entered the lane. The driver slammed on the brakes, raised the front wheel in the air, and barely missed her. Hearing of these accidents, my constant prayer became, "God, please watch over my children and protect them."

One day when I came home from work, I found four eggs in a bowl on the table. *How wonderful,* I thought. *We'll have scrambled eggs tonight.* "Who gave us this gift?" I asked the children.

"I found them," Agnes beamed, "under the hedge there."

"You found a nest?"

She nodded, her face dimpled in a happy smile. Always the practical one, she was pleased to be able to make a contribution to our supper. I hated to disappoint her, but I knew we couldn't keep the eggs.

"Agnes, do the chickens belong to us?" I asked.

She shook her head no. "Well, then, the eggs they lay do not belong to us either," I said softly. "Come, we'll take them back now." Ludwig, the manager of the rooming house, looked surprised when I handed him the eggs, but he understood why it was important for him to keep them.

There were other opportunities to teach the children about respecting other people's property. Behind the barn was a woodpile which the other inhabitants used, but since I hadn't been invited to do so, I didn't feel right about helping myself to it. Often on a summer evening, the girls and I combed the forest for pine cones and brushwood. When our sacks were full and we had several bundles of brushwood tied up with a rope, we dragged them home and stacked them in the barn. It was hard, scratchy work but the girls were good sports about it.

Where Are All My People?

For the first time in many months, life became almost normal for us in Austria. We enjoyed our own place. Granted, it was only one room in a rooming house with bars across the windows; still, we thought it was grand. I earned enough food for the children and they were happy in school and other activities. I had nothing to complain about and yet, I was desperately lonely. I longed for fellowship with my own people. Where was my husband? All my searching through the Red Cross produced nothing. And how about all my relatives and friends? Was I the only survivor?

One night, it must have been near morning, I fell into a fitful sleep. Moments later, I heard a sharp knocking on the window. I pulled back the curtain and gasped. Isaac stood at the window wearing a hooded jacket; the hood was untied and trimmed with brown fur. His grey eyes, brimming with sadness, looked out of a thin, pale face. His sunken cheeks were unshaven. "Neta, are you going to let me come in?" he asked quietly.

"Oh, Isaac, you've come back," I cried.

I jumped out of bed. Not bothering to put my slippers on, I hurried to open the door.

I pushed it open wide, expecting my husband's strong embrace.

Isaac was gone.

When I awoke, my body was damp with perspiration. "Oh, Isaac, where have you gone?" I sobbed.

Nobody seemed to know what really happened to my husband. All I had been told was that in a surprise tank attack at night, Isaac's battalion had been wiped out. It was likely that some soldiers had escaped, but nobody knew for certain. It was too dangerous to return and retrieve the bodies. Still, Isaac was declared missing, not dead. And so, a flame of hope kept me searching.

Early one morning, I walked to a refugee camp in Reid, a small town not far from Eggerding. A large group of refugees from Ukraine had arrived, and it could be that some of my people were among them. As I neared the camp, my excitement grew. Perhaps today I would find somebody from our village, maybe even a relative. But the camp was filled with strangers who didn't even speak German. Not a single person I knew, nor a single lead to my family. Disappointed, I returned to Eggerding, my head pounding with a ferocious migraine. I gave the children their supper, then crawled into bed and pulled the covers over me. A short while later, Frau Wiesmeier surprised me with a visit. She sat down beside my bed and asked me about my trip. I told her about my fruitless search. "The Red Cross can't find Isaac," I choked. "And I don't know where the others are. Maybe all the people I'm searching for have died." My friend didn't say much; she just listened. Later, she brought me an aspirin and a cup of hot tea.

Go Back to Russia

One afternoon, a municipal clerk brought me a letter from the government. Fear bolted through me. What did they want? Quickly, I tore open the letter. "The war is over," I read. "We will arrange transportation for you to return to your home in Ukraine. Be ready in two days." The room began to swim before me and I grabbed the table to steady myself. By now I had fancied myself safe in the American sector, but even here the long arm of the Russians had found me. All night I tossed in my bed. Will the Austrians be glad to be rid of me and my children? I knew that some, like the shoemaker's wife, wanted to evict every refugee in their country. Who would believe me that for me to go back was the same as suicide? "Oh, God help me," I prayed. "I have nobody to turn to."

The next morning, I walked to the bürgermeister's office. As I entered, he beckoned for me to sit down. But I remained standing.

"I'm not going back to Russia," I said.

"You're not going home?" he looked puzzled.

"The Russians won't send me home; they'll send me to Siberia." My voice began to quaver and I fought a lump rising in my throat. I steeled myself and stood tall—I would not resort to crying and begging. "If you want to get rid of me so badly," I shouted, "you can shoot me. Now!"

The bürgermeister looked alarmed. "Frau Loewen, nobody wants to hurt you."

160

My impassioned speech reached the ears of an American officer in the next room. He came to see what all the commotion was about. Soon I was telling them about my Mennonite history: how our ancestors seeking religious freedom immigrated to Russia during the reign of Catherine the Great; how the communists took away our freedom, our houses and our lands; how we lived near starvation while harvesting rich crops of grain; and how many of my relatives were either murdered or banished to Siberia simply for their German heritage or their Mennonite faith.

"That's what they will do with me," I concluded. "They will put my children into a state orphanage and send me to a labour camp in Siberia."

The bürgermeister translated my words into English, and the American officer listened intently. When I finished speaking, the two men held a brief conference, then the bürgermeister said, "Frau Loewen, you and your children may stay in Austria. The Americans will protect you." He walked me to the door and shook my hand. "If ever you need anything, feel free to come to me. I will do everything I can to help you."

Greatly relieved, I returned home. But at night, doubts began to plague me. Did I do the right thing by refusing to go back? Herr and Frau Dührer and the children were going back to eastern Germany. Maybe all our Mennonite people were returning to our native villages in Ukraine and I was here alone with my children. But no, we had risked all for freedom; surely my relatives would not go back voluntarily. If they were still alive, they must be here in the west. I would keep searching for them.

An Austrian Christmas (1945)

One day in November, the houseparents with the orphan children returned to East Germany. Before they left, Frau Dührer, gave me two pieces of beautiful fabric. *Just in time for Christmas,* I thought. While the children slept, I sewed dresses for my two oldest girls, a shirt for Fred, and a rag doll for Katie. By Christmas Eve, everything was ready. I waited for the children to fall asleep, then I placed three hard candies and an apple onto each plate, and laid the clothes and the doll beside the plates. I stepped back and surveyed the beautiful table.

How wonderful to be able to celebrate Christmas again, I thought. And yet, I was very lonely tonight. Just outside our windows I heard footsteps crunching on the snow and low muffled voices of families going to midnight mass. I wiped away tears as I remembered Christmases past surrounded by loved ones. Would I ever see them again?

A sudden knocking on the door made me jump. Who could be coming at this hour? Cautiously, I opened the door.

"Merry Christmas, Frau Loewen," two girls chimed. "We've brought you a Christmas tree."

I stared at the small tree, beautifully decorated. "You've done this for *me*?"

The Wiesmeier girls giggled. "Mother also sends this," they said as they handed me a bag of cookies and two picture books. After the girls' brief visit, my spirits lifted. *I'm far from home, yet among friends,* I thought. I crawled into bed beside Lena and was soon fast asleep.

What a joyful Christmas morning! My children's eyes shone as they gazed at the Christmas tree and then at the presents on the table. Katie hugged her doll and promptly christened her Katarina. The girls giggled as they modelled their new dresses. Fred was soon lost in a new picture book.

A Village School

Just across the yard from our rooming house, beside an apple orchard, was the school building. Now emptied of straw, refurbished, and fully functional, it seemed strange to think of it as a former refugee camp. Fräulein Zendron, a refugee from Czechoslovakia, took teaching our children very seriously. She insisted on hard work, good penmanship, and a neat page. There were no text books. A tabloid-style reader printed on cheap paper in Linz, Austria, arrived several times a year. It carried short stories, poems and songs of the season; also Grimm's fairy tales and Austrian folklore. On the back page were the following words: "American soldiers are now living with us. They are speaking English. We want to understand what they are saying. That is why we are trying to learn English." A vocabulary of English words followed along with popular phrases such as: "Good morning! Where's your pass? Okay. Please, sir, give me some chocolate. Thank you. Good-bye." There followed an instruction on how to hold your tongue so that you would pronounce the "th" softly.

Painstakingly, Lena and Agnes practised writing the letters of the alphabet in the Austrian style. Since paper was scarce, the girls practised in the margin of a newspaper or on a piece of scrap paper. Only the best handwriting went into a scribbler. To conserve space, no margins were allowed. Neatness was prized above all. Lacking an eraser, some children tried to rub out a mistake by licking a finger and rubbing it across the word. A smudge formed which occasioned a severe reprimand from the teacher. My girls took delight in their studies; they read every available book in the school library, memorized poetry, learned German folk songs, and enjoyed educational field trips. One such trip took them into local fields looking for potato bugs. On a bright, sunny May morning, Fräulein Zendron lined up the children in neat marching rows. As they walked out of the school yard, I heard them singing, *"Der Mai ist gekommen, die Bäume schlagen aus"* (May has come and trees are bursting at the seams). A prize awaited the child who found the most potato bugs: a new pencil or a scribbler. I marvelled at the dedication of the children's teacher–nothing seemed to be too much work for her. When Lena announced one day that her class was going to make a trip up one of northern Austria's Pre-Alps, I tried to gently inform her, that, since we had no money, she would not be going. But, Fräulein Zendron wouldn't hear of it. The money was somehow provided, and Lena got to go along with her classmates. A trip to the Feuerkogel (1592 metres) was no small undertaking. The children travelled by train, by boat across the Ebensee, and finally up the mountain in a gondola. Lena was brimming with news when she came home: They'd slept in an Alpine hut–just like Heidi—and early the next morning, they'd been awakened by the clanging of cow bells as the *Sennerin* took the cows to pasture. She brought home a small bouquet of Alpine flowers which she had picked for me.

When Fred was six, he began first grade. On the first day of school, not being used to sitting still so long, he came running home during lunch hour declaring, "I've had enough education." But soon Fräulein Zendron had won his heart, and he liked going to school. One day his little sister decided to follow her brother. The teacher took pity on the little waif standing in the doorway of the classroom, peering around longingly. She invited Katie to come into the classroom, showed her to a seat, then gave her some "work" to do. But Fred's humiliation was keen: "Don't ever do that again," he admonished his sister sternly. And she never did.

A Surprise Birthday Party

In the summer of 1946, while I worked in Bramberger's fields, my two girls schemed a secret birthday party for me. They wanted to present me with a birthday cake, so they spoke to Frau Wiesmeier about it. "I'll bake it," she said, "if you girls can bring me all the ingredients."

Quickly, Lena jotted down what would be needed: two eggs, flour, sugar, butter, cocoa...Of course, my girls didn't have money, and our small rations from the store didn't include such luxuries. But the girls were determined.

"We'll go hamstering," Agnes said.

Soon the girls tramped the countryside. At a formidable door, the two whispered anxiously: "Your turn this time"; "no, I did it last time, your turn." Then overcoming fear, the appointed spokesperson knocked. "We want to give our mother a birthday cake," she began. "Please, would you have an egg to spare?"

Austrian farmers responded with cheer and goodwill; they also kept the girls' secret.

On my thirty-fourth birthday, when I came home from work, a beautiful chocolate cake graced our table. Four excited children hopped around it and chimed, "Happy Birthday, Mother!" Then Fred piped up, "Cut it, Mommy," followed by little Katie's urging, "Can we eat it now?"

What a feast we had! It was the ultimate treat for children who'd known nothing more than boiled potatoes, dark rye bread, and the occasional cooky at Christmas time. For many days afterward, Austrians who had donated to the cake wished me a "Happy Birthday."

In so many ways, my Austrian neighbours surprised me with kindness. One day, while doing laundry, I cut my finger badly and it became infected. Soon my entire hand became red and swollen and extremely painful. Towards evening, red streaks crept up my arm. When I showed Frau Schmolz, she became alarmed. "Blood poisoning," she said, "we've got to act quickly." There was no doctor in Eggerding and I had no transportation to make the trip to Schärding where there was one. My friend heated a black salve on the stove, then made a compress for my hand. She stayed the night with me, changing the dressing every two hours, and offering me herbal tea. She probably saved my life.

One of the people I did odd jobs for was the local Catholic priest. A high brown wooden fence divided his garden from our front yard with its enormous linden tree. In the summer, the neighbourhood children played in a sandpile under the tree. I'm sure they disturbed the vicar's nap, for at times he would holler out of his window, "Quiet, children."

My girls went with their Austrian friends to the Roman Catholic Church. Frau Marklin often worried aloud about the fact that my children were not baptized. Lena, who's heart was tender towards God, sometimes begged me to allow her to be baptized into the Roman Catholic faith.

"Wait until you have visited other churches," I said to her.

"But I'll go straight to hell when I die." Her blue eyes filled with worry. "Hansi says so."

"I disagree with Hansi," I said. "God loves you, and He knows you love Him."

Little incidents like this made me long for my own people. Although Catholic theology was different from our Mennonite faith, I was glad for the religious instruction my children received through the local church. How I loved to hear the bells tolling from the church tower! You could hear the melodious sound for miles around. There were different bells for different occasions. On Good Friday—to commemorate the suffering and death of Christ—no bells sounded from the tower. On Easter Sunday, *all* the bells rang out proclaiming the happy news, "Christ is risen!"Agnes and Lena loved to watch the bell ringers. Sometimes the boys would let them have a try at the ropes.

One spring day, after a thunderstorm, as Lena went outside, she heard a "cheep, cheep"coming from underneath a pear tree. She hurried over. Three baby starlings with mottled feathers were hopping on the wet ground. A black tomcat pounced upon the birds and carried off one little victim in its mouth. Lena sprinted over and scooped up the other two starlings. Their little hearts beat wildly against her cupped fingers. She brought them inside our home and fixed a "nest" for them in a cardboard box. When I came home from work, she begged me to allow her to keep the birds.

"But you must look after them."

She nodded her head.

The following morning one of the starlings had died. The other one was very much alive: he cocked his downy head and looked at us with bright, black eyes. Eagerly, he swallowed the flies and drops of water the children gave him. Day after day, the bird grew and gained strength and courage. He climbed out of his cardboard nest and sat on the rung of a chair, peering at us with his saucy, little eyes. Then he'd spread his wings and attempt a short flight–from his perch to the wash stand, then to the bed and the window sill. Each time he'd look at us as though he were expecting applause. So applaud we did! I was pleased the children had found a pet which gave them so much joy. It was a bit disconcerting, though, to have the bird jump on the table and pick off our plates during meal times. I was also not too pleased about the messes he made on the floor. Sometimes I was tempted to tell the children the time had come for the bird to leave, but I didn't have the heart; they enjoyed his company so much.

The bird made our children instant celebrities. Lena would go for walks outside with "Hansi" (as she called him) perched on her right index finger. The bird would leave her finger and fly into a nearby cherry tree. She allowed for a few minutes of feeding time, then she'd call, "Hansi!" With a delightful chirp, he'd swoop down and land on her index finger again. At the post office, the bird would jump down onto the counter and peer at the clerk through the grate as though he'd come to say "Hello."All the children in the village wanted to hold him. In exchange they supplied dead flies and worms for Hansi's feeding.

Fall days tinged the leaves golden and put a nip in the air. Birds gathered in swarms, sagging the electric wires. And Hansi got restless. One day he left his perch on Lena's finger and soared into the open sky to join a swarm of starlings on the barn roof. This time, no amount of calling brought him back. Lena cried bitterly. "He's with his own now," I tried to console her. "That's where he belongs." But a sadness filled my heart also. *When will I be able to say I'm with my own ?* I wondered. All my searching for my loved ones had turned up nothing.

So the seasons came and went. Another winter came to Eggerding and the snow blanketed the trees and hills. Austrian children shared their toboggans with my children and they spent many happy hours sliding down the hillside together. Toward evening, they returned home with sparkling eyes and rosy cheeks and huge appetites.

Christmas celebrations came early to Eggerding–on the evening of December 5th—with a visit from St. Nicholas and Grampus. Dressed in a bishop's cloak and a tall hat, St. Nicholas carried a staff and a small bag of goodies. Grampus, resembling a black devil, wore a scary mask with horns and a long red tongue. He carried a wooden stick and a chain to threaten children who misbehaved. Rumour had it, that Grampus chained up naughty children to a tree and left them there all night. Well, my children were taking no chances. At the sight of him, they ducked for cover—Lena and Agnes under the table and Fred and Katie behind my back. "Have the children been good?" St. Nicholas asked in a sonorous voice.

"Yes, they've been good and helpful," I said, whereupon St. Nicholas reached into his bag and retrieved four cookies; then he coaxed the children to come and get them. Turning to leave, Grampus rattled his chain once more, in warning or, perhaps, in disappointment that his services were not needed.

The following day, Lena told me how the boys at school teased her. "You should have seen her hide under the table," a big boy laughed. He made a face and, crouching low, he hugged his head. Having everyone laugh at her was unpleasant, of course, but suddenly Lena's face brightened. "You were Grampus?" (Apparently, older school boys played the role around town.) With this revelation, a bit of Lena's childhood innocence evaporated.

Agnes, also, made an important discovery that Christmas. Several weeks before Christmas, Katie's doll had disappeared. The girls looked everywhere, but couldn't find her. Come Christmas morning, a new Raggedy Anne lay beside Katie's plate. A fresh new face looked out of a mop of red hair. She wore an apron over a pretty little dress, a slip, and pantaloons down to her ankles. Agnes picked up the doll and examined her closely. As she lifted up the dress and the petticoat, and pulled back the panties, her eyes lit up. She walked over and whispered in my ear, "It's the same doll, right?" We smiled at our secret.

Looking For A Country

The International Refugee Organization, stationed in Linz, Austria, sent me a letter urging me to make application for immigration. To make the trip to and from the IRO office took me one very long day. Early in the morning, I walked to Andorf and then took a train to Linz. After I filled out the immigration papers to Canada, the clerk said, "Next time, bring your children."

"I have no transportation," I said.

"We can't proceed with your application unless your children are examined by our doctors," she said. What was I to do? Though my girls could walk the nine kilometre distance to the train station, six-year-old Fred and four-year old Katie could not do it. Dejectedly, I returned to Eggerding. Immigration would have to wait.

One day, as I was mulling over our future–I knew in crowded Austria we had no future–immigration seemed very appealing. Suddenly, I remembered a neighbour who delivered bread to the train station in Andorf three days a week. Perhaps, if he took along Fred and Katie, we could make a trip to Linz after all. He readily agreed, and on the appointed day, I bundled up Katie and Fred in their warmest clothing and sent them along with the bread wagon. "When you get to the train station," I instructed, "go inside where it's warm and wait for me." Meanwhile, the girls and I walked. Everything went according to plan and soon all of us were boarding a train to Linz. I was glad I'd insisted on warm winter clothing, for it was quite cold in our car. At one place, the train stopped and a conductor came into our car to check tickets. "Folks, move to the front," he said. "The first three cars are heated. " Hurriedly, all the passengers exited and made the transfer, but the children and I, walking alongside the train, made slow progress. We were still walking to the front when the train began to move. I yelled for my children to get onto the train. Lena made the jump, then, clutching Katie to myself, I grabbed the handle bar and pulled ourselves on board. "*Ach, Gott!*" (Good, God!) a conductor hollered and pulled me inside. Katie and Lena were with me, but where were Agnes and Fred?

"Stupid woman," the conductor scolded.

"Stop the train," I gasped. "My children–"

But the conductor had already moved to the next car. The train was going full-speed now. I was frantic with worry. Had Fred and Agnes managed to get themselves onto the train? No, they were too young. Why hadn't I stayed where I was? I should have known that the children and I wouldn't be able to reach the car in time. Now my worst nightmare had come to pass: I'd lost some of my children!

"Stop the train," I shouted. "My children–my children are left behind." A stunned silence hung over the passengers. What were they to make of this woman? Was she insane? What mother would leave her children behind? One man shouted, "Get off at the next stop."

Suddenly, a conductor entered our car bringing Agnes and Fred with him.

"Mama!" They rushed towards me.

Tears of relief streamed down my face as I hugged my children close to me. "You're a lucky woman," the conductor said. Realizing our predicament, he had hoisted Agnes and Fred into a passing car, then he had hopped into a car behind theirs. Now he was walking from car to car trying to find the parents. Thank God, I had my children back with me, but my mind conjured up all sorts of "what ifs" and I kept condemning myself for my carelessness.

At nine that evening, we finally arrived in Linz. We found lodging in a building across from the train station in a large room filled with people. Soon the children were sound asleep, but I was too worked up to sleep. In time, exhaustion overpowered me, but as soon as I dozed off, I was tormented by dreams of losing my children. I heard the clickety-clack of a fast-moving train. I saw my children dangling from the hand railing, swaying wildly with the movement of the train. I must have screamed in my sleep for a woman shook me awake and told me to be quiet. I fought sleep but I couldn't keep myself awake. Again, I dreamt. I saw my children thrashing about wildly in a big lake. I grabbed Agnes by her red hair, but she slipped away from me and went under. Again, I screamed. A sharp poke in my ribs awoke me. This time I got out of bed and took a chair by the window. Better to sit up the remainder of the night than to risk another nightmare.

After breakfast, a van came to take us and some other refugees to the IRO office. A woman, wearing a beautiful fur coat, took Katie on her lap. She was quite taken by my little girl with the wispy, blond hair and spoke kindly to her. Suddenly, Katie's little face got very pale and her huge eyes flashed me a distress signal: "I'm going to be sick, Mama." But before I could reach her, she heaved her breakfast all over the woman's fur coat. Of course, I apologized, but the damage was done.

An IRO doctor gave me and each of the children a thorough physical examination. Passport photos were taken, and then I was given another detailed questionnaire to fill out. I was stumped at the question, "Give the full name and address of your sponsor." I didn't have a sponsor. I knew my mother had cousins in Canada somewhere but I didn't know where and I didn't know if they would sponsor us. I filled out the application the best I could and handed it in.

Our return trip to Eggerding was uneventful. We arrived home in the dark and I was very grateful when all of us were safe in our little room again. Many months went by and nothing came of my application to immigrate. In all that time I didn't meet a single person from our home in Ukraine. I began to wonder if we were the last surviving Mennonites in Europe.

Meanwhile Eggerding began to feel more like home to us. I made some very good friends. I continued to work hard and my girls also helped out. During the summer, Bramberger hired them to carry apple cider to his field hands. For this service, they earned a free meal. They also herded cows for the Mühlböcks for additional food. My friend, the bürgermeister, gave me a pailful of flour in exchange for berries the children and I picked. So in various ways, we got enough food to eat.

The Lost Is Found

One evening, I went to water the plants in a small garden plot Bramberger gave me for personal use. On the way, I met a young man carrying a black briefcase. I could tell at a glance that he was a stranger in our village.

"Guten Abend," he said in accented German, "I'm looking for Frau Loewen."

"That's me," I said hesitantly.

"My name is Arthur Voth—from America," he smiled. "May I talk with you."

Why? What do you want? My mind raced.

I invited him into our home and offered him a glass of milk.

"You are a Mennonite from Ukraine, aren't you?"

My heart skipped a beat. Why was he asking? "Yes, I'm a Mennonite," I said, " the only one in Austria."

173

"No, there are many," he said, "but they don't live near you." He told me he'd come from America and was working with the Mennonite Central Committee (MCC) to find displaced persons scattered throughout Austria. "Our aim is to reconnect families," he said. "Are you missing anyone?"

"I'm missing *all* my family," I blurted. I was trembling so hard, I had to sit down. *Can this man really help me?*

Arthur lifted a scribbler out of his briefcase, "Give me some names."

"Isaac Loewen, my husband."

He scanned his list of names beginning with "L", but after a few tense moments, he shook his head no. "Sorry, he's not in my book," he said. "But I have Helena Loewen and her daughter, Lena."

"My husband's mother and sister," I cried. "What about my mother, Anganetha Dyck?"

"Anganetha Dyck in Treffling," he said slowly. "Does she have a daughter Tina? Tina Vogt who has a son named Victor?"

"That's my sister," I said. "What about Annie Dyck?"

"Sorry, no mention of Annie Dyck."

Arthur continued to search for names I gave him and soon he found several of my relatives, also my friends Anna Harder and Sarah Harder.

"What about Franz Harder?" I asked.

"He died while his family was in Czechoslovakia staying in a refugee camp," Arthur said. Thank God, Franz had survived the trek then! My heart went out to Anna—she'd miss him terribly. And his infant son would never get to know his father. In my mind's eye, I could still hear Franz's desperate plea on that dark winter night in Poland four years ago, "For God's sake, take along this woman and her children." Franz had gone from wagon to wagon until he'd found a farmer who'd taken along Sarah and five of her children; the oldest two children had been picked up by another wagon. *Franz has received his wish,* I thought, *both his family and Sarah's family are safe.* And God had answered my prayer and helped me find my loved ones again. Quickly, I jotted down addresses.

As Arthur prepared to leave, he promised to keep in touch. He also gave me a card which entitled me to pick up a care package in Linz once a month.

"Our heavenly Father sent you today," I said in parting.

"Yes, I believe that too." He shook my hand and left.

In the evening, I wrote my mother in Treffling, an Austrian town in the English zone. I found it difficult to express my joy at having found her and Tina, but I was worried about my youngest sister, Annie. Why wasn't she with them? What had happened to her?

A week later, a letter arrived from my mother. She was overjoyed to hear from me and to know we were well. Tina and Victor were living with her in a refugee camp with many other Mennonites. Annie had become separated from them at the Yugoslavian/Austrian border when partisans had ordered her off the truck. The last time they saw her, she was in a group of young people marching back into enemy territory.

The events that unravelled in the following weeks were so remarkable that I often had to stop and ask myself, "Is this real or am I dreaming?"

In late fall, Tina came to visit me in Eggerding. She brought clothes for each of my children, but they were too small. "Your children have grown so much," she laughed. We talked and talked until late into the night. I wanted to know every detail of their experiences, so I plied my sister with questions.

"On October 5th, 1943, we left Nieder-Chortitza by train,"Tina began. "Grandmother, Tante Anna, Mother, Annie, Victor, and I left in a group of 163 persons, mostly older women or young women with small children. We did not make much progress, what with frequent stops to repair rails and bridges. In Sereowka, a small town on the Ukrainian steppes, German soldiers ordered us off the train. We were surrounded by Russians! We found shelter in houses near the railway station. We stayed for two weeks, waiting for the Germans to break through the barricade. During this time, Grandmother died. Quickly, we called together friends and former neighbours for a Christian funeral. The singing around her grave side sounded like a choir. It was wonderful, Neta." Tina's eyes grew misty. "I was sad to know our grandmother was gone, but happy too, that we were able to give her a Christian burial. But for the barricade, we would have been on the road and there would not have been time to bury her."

Tina and I sat silently, pondering the mysterious workings of God.

"Tell me about Annie," I said. "How did you get separated?"

"We were in Yugoslavia when the war ended," Tina began. "We wanted to get out of a communist country as soon as possible. So we joined the hordes of people who were making their way to the Yugoslavian/Austrian border, some on foot, some in jeeps. When we got to the border, the border patrol wouldn't let us pass. Annie and I were told to get off the jeep and join a group of German soldiers and young civilians. With a start I realized they were making us prisoners-of-war. From the back of the jeep, I heard Victor crying softly for his mother. But what could I do? Suddenly my mother yelled in platt deutsch, 'Tina, get over here. Your child needs you.' With the sound of her voice ringing in my ears, it seemed more important to obey my mother than those gun-wielding partisans. I left the group, jumped back onto the jeep, and hugged my child."

"Force of habit," I laughed. As children we hadn't dared to disobey Mother. Still, her no-nonsense approach had often saved us from serious trouble.

"But Annie wasn't so fortunate," Tina continued. "As far as we know, she's somewhere in Yugoslavia as a prisoner-of-war."

"How did you and Mother get across the border then?" I asked.

"The partisans took away the jeeps and we had to walk. A kind farmer gave me a little wagon and I put our luggage and Victor into it. But we made slow progress. Soon everybody passed us and then we were all alone. We were always in danger of being captured or shot. One day we entered a village and saw, to our great relief, that the soldiers were not wearing a communist uniform. We had safely arrived in the English zone. The soldiers supplied a truck and took us and some other refugees to a displaced person's camp in Klagenfurt. When the weather turned cold, they transported us to the present camp in Treffling. It's not a bad camp," Tina concluded, "the rooms are heated and the food is good. Besides, I'm able to earn a little money by doing laundry for English soldiers. That's how I could afford a bus trip to come see you now."

A few months after Tina's visit, I received the welcome news that Annie had joined them. Soon Annie wrote me a letter.

In the march back into Yugoslavia, I was wounded in both of my legs and left beside the road to die. But two men, driving an oxen cart, came along and picked me up and took me to a hospital. A German doctor, also a prisoner-of-war like myself, operated on my legs, and because of his excellent care, I can walk again. When the Russians threatened to send me back to Ukraine, this dear doctor smuggled me out of Yugoslavia into Austria. I owe my life to him! For over a year, I kept searching for my family, and I'm so grateful to have found them at last. God has done incredible things for me, Neta. I won't go into detail now, but I'll tell you all about it when we meet again. I hope it's soon." (For more of Annie's story, see the Appendix)

Farewell to Austria

One Sunday afternoon in 1947, Arthur Voth and Vandenberg, another MCC worker, came to visit me. They told me that many of our Mennonite people were immigrating to Canada, U.S.A., or Paraguay and they wondered if I was interested.

"Yes, I am," I said and told them about my unsuccessful trip to the IRO office two winters ago.

"We must move you to an MCC camp in Germany," Vandenberg said. "That's the first step towards immigration." Then he asked me if I had any relatives in Canada.

"My mother has a cousin in British Columbia," I said. "But I don't have an address."

Spring came again to Eggerding. One day, Frau Mühlböck announced they were going to renovate the old house, and while this was going on, we would have to move out. But where to?

"Frau Loewen, I'll give you Schmied's room," Bramberger said. "You've worked for me all these years."

I knew Frau Schmied's husband had been killed in the war, leaving her with five children to support. *Kick her out so I can have a room?* I thought. No, I would not do that!

"That's kind of you, Herr Bramberger," I said. "But I already have a place. *Dear God, forgive my lie and please help me find a place.* The renovation was to begin at the other end of the house so I wouldn't have to move immediately. That gave me some comfort.

The renovation also provided another job for me. As walls were being torn down, old bricks were scraped so they could be used again in reconstruction. One Friday, the third week in June 1948, I was scraping away at bricks in the sweltering sun. I was hot, dusty, and tired. *Just like the children of Israel,* I thought, *I'm working with bricks in a foreign country.* Then I laughed. Nobody was standing over me with a whip demanding an outrageous quota. It was a poor comparison. At about three o-clock in the afternoon, a mailman found me at the brick pile. "Frau Loewen, a telegram," he said. I put down my hammer, rubbed my dusty hands on my skirt, and opened the telegram.

Linz, Austria
June 17, 1948 at 1615
    Concerning a move to Backnang, Germany. Be ready Sunday morning with children and baggage. I'll pick you up early. M.C.C. Vandenberg.

I dropped the hammer and hurried into my home to pack. In a few minutes Resl came to look for me and I gave her the telegram to read. Later, Frau Mühlböck also came to visit.

"Are you really leaving us?" she asked.

"Yes," I said.

"Why? Your girls will soon be old enough to work in my store. You could have a good life here." She looked down at her hands for a moment. "At first, I didn't want anything to do with you," she said, her face reddening slightly.

"You must understand, we were bitterly disappointed by refugees." Then she brightened. "But you have not disappointed us. You have worked hard for us. Ludwig speaks of you with the highest regard." When I looked surprised, she laughed. "I know about you returning the eggs." Her eyes twinkled merrily. "Agnes, you have many friends here," she concluded. "I hope you will reconsider your decision."

I thanked her kindly, then added, "I want to be with my own people."

In the evening, another friend came to say good-bye. "Who will do my washing and cleaning for me?" she asked. "I have nobody I can trust like you."

The next morning, a truck came to pick us up. It was raining hard, but even so, a group of friends and neighbours gathered on the yard to see us off. Even the priest stood in the rain without a hat. As he shook my hand, he stuffed some schillings into my hand. Frau Marklin and Frau Schmolz wept unashamedly. It was hard to say good-bye to these kind people who had been my family for the past three years.

CHAPTER TWELVE

Refugee Camps in Western Germany (1948-1949)

A TRUCK TOOK US to the train station in Linz and we joined a small group of refugees, Mennonites like us, on the way to an MCC refugee camp in Germany. One woman's face looked very familiar and I puzzled as to where I might have seen her. Suddenly, it dawned on me: Maria, a friend from Nieder-Chortitza! But when I greeted her, she said, "Do I know you?"

I was stunned. I began to explain our connection, but Maria acted like she didn't want to hear about it. This really puzzled me. Soon all thirty-two of us crammed into a boxcar with a huge Red Cross on it. I pushed our luggage into a corner and told the children to sit on top of it. When evening came, we mothers prepared to spread blankets on the floor for our children to sleep on. "Just a minute," Maria's husband said. "This half of the train is for my family." He gestured to the other half. "That's where you sleep." Soon his family was comfortably stretched out in *his* half of the car, while the rest of us squeezed into the other half. All night, I sat up holding Katie on my lap because there wasn't enough floor space to lie down. *How ironic*, I thought. *Here I am with my people and they treat me like this.*

The next morning, my children and I moved to a passenger car. Because there were only a few people in the car, some benches were empty, so we could lie down and go to sleep. We stayed there for the rest of the journey. Total strangers shared their food with us.

I could not change my money at the Austrian border because inflation had rendered the Austrian schilling worthless. I handed all my savings to the custom's officer and told him to give it to the Red Cross. Later, when we arrived at the MCC refugee camp in Sulzbach, Germany, I received 40 Deutsche mark per person for spending money. The refugee camp was a converted school building. A large classroom was divided into many cubicles by suspending grey army blankets from wires that criss-crossed the room. Behind a blanketed cubicle stood two bunk-beds on either side of a wooden crate which held all our worldly possessions. That became our new home.

Living behind blankets in such close quarters held its challenges. One could inadvertently eavesdrop on people's conversations and hear what one wasn't prepared to hear. One day Lena heard her name mentioned on the other side of the blanket. A boy was telling his mother how ridiculous she had looked standing in front of the church–on a little platform, no less–while everybody sang "Happy Birthday!" to her. Lena's cheeks flushed and she looked at me in confusion. My twelve-year-old, even though she was unusually tall for her age, was still very much a child at heart. She'd seen nothing wrong with the teacher's request. Now, she began to doubt herself. Was she too grown up for such childish things? Confused, she became moody and argumentative.

Going to the bathroom at night presented another problem. In the dark one had to find one's way through a maze of blanketed cubicles to the hall. It happened on occasion that somebody became disoriented on the way back and crawled into the wrong bed. This was always looked upon as a big joke. But when Agnes complained, "Mom, that big boy let's me see him naked," I was worried, and I moved her off the top bunk to the bottom bunk.

One night I felt a big hand touching my arm through the blanket-wall. Then the hand pushed in further and began to grope my body. I pushed the hand away, got out of bed, and moved Katie next to the blanket. I figured he would not molest a little child.

In this overcrowded refugee camp, there wasn't much activity planned for children to do. We adults had our chores and chat groups, but the children were free to roam. We looked forward to Saturdays when local soccer teams battled it out on the field behind the school. This provided a lot of entertainment for young and old alike. One day, Fred climbed a fence, to see the game better; he lost his footing, and crashed to the ground. Agnes came running with the news, "Fred's hurt—badly." I followed Agnes to the place where my young son lay on the ground. Seeing the large swelling on his right forearm and how the lower arm and hand hung at an unnatural angle, I guessed it was serious. Someone called a first-aid worker who arranged a ride for Fred and me to a hospital in Backnang near Stuttgart.

Fred was hospitalized in a room with three men. His right arm was put into traction, and for three weeks my eight-year-old son was unable to leave his bed. But he had excellent roommates who kept him amused with little stories and good-natured teasing. "Where did you come from?" One man asked him. When Fred said "Sulzbach," his roommate replied, "Oh, that's far away—on the outer edge of the world." I walked the 12.5 km distance every other day, and seeing Fred happy, was a great relief to me. It also made me realize how much Fred missed male company. He had never known the company of his father, nor that of his uncles. They had all vanished either in Stalin's purges or during the war.

I was delighted when the following week we moved to the MCC refugee camp in Backnang, near Stuttgart. The buildings consisted of a row of barracks and a leather tannery on the edge of town. From there, I walked to the hospital every day. When Fred was discharged, he still couldn't straighten his arm. But the nurse handed him a brown bag with a brick in it. "You must carry this for half an hour three times a day," she told him. (Even today, Fred cannot straighten his right arm completely, nor can he touch his shoulder, but he tells me, it's not hampering him in any way.)

About this time, my mother and siblings, along with their families, also moved to Backnang. What a happy reunion we had! Five long years of separation melted away. And yet, they'd left their mark on us. I was shocked to see how my mother had aged; her hair had turned white and her face was etched in deep wrinkles. Annie's wounds had healed, and, despite ugly scars, she was walking with only a slight limp. "An absolute miracle," she told me. At one time, the doctor had talked about amputation. Tina was in good spirits despite the fact that, like me, she had absolutely no news of David her husband. I couldn't believe how much Victor had grown. *But then, we usually see the biggest change in our children,* I reflected. All nine of us moved into one room, sharing four bunk beds. At mealtime, my sister and I would fetch our ration of food from a communal kitchen and then we would gather round a small table in our room.

Our meal times were noisy and enjoyable–there was so much catching up to do.

In Backnang, as well as in other MCC camps where we spent time, there were programs for young and old alike. Adults were assigned to various chores to help keep the camp running smoothly: Mother and I worked in the kitchen while Annie and Tina taught in kindergarten. Our children were happily engaged in various programs. Besides regular school hours throughout the week, there was Sunday school and worship services and a children's choir. I was pleased when Lena and Agnes were chosen to sing a duet during an evening service. "*In dem Himmel ist's wunderschön*," (heaven is a wonderful place) they sang in harmony but feeling shy, they kept looking down at the floor.

"Girls, you must look at the people," I told them.

"I'm too scared!" Agnes said.

"Pretend you're singing to me."

Scripture memory competitions on a Sunday night provided another challenge. Two opposing teams would face each other. A child from team "A" would recite a Bible verse, then a child from team "B". The following rules applied: 1) A different verse each time; 2) If you were stuck, you sat down; and 3) The winning team was the one with a person still standing. If the winner could come up with a verse which had not yet been recited, the child received extra points. The children enjoyed this very much. They also received lessons in practical skills such as crafts for the girls and woodworking for the boys. My girls learned how to embroider, crochet, knit and weave. The teachers also organized programs for Christmas and Easter and other special occasions.

I remember a Spring Festival on the meadow. The parents (mostly mothers) were sitting on the grass. The sun was shining, a sweet fragrance hung in the air, and a gentle breeze caressed our cheeks. Lena and Agnes, dressed in daffodil yellow, were holding an arbour covered with vines. Other flower-clad children formed a circle around a gaggle of green-clad frogs—Katie and Fred among them– who hopped about and croaked, "Coooo-wack–wack-wack. Coooo-wack-wack-wack."

Seeing my children so happily engaged gave me great joy; coupled with the fact that I was now with my own people. Still, I was worried about our future. For lack of a sponsor and because I did not qualify as a worker, Canada had rejected my application for immigration. Many refugees, including my mother's sister, Tante Anna, were going to Paraguay, so I decided I, too, would apply for Paraguay. One day, I went to the MCC office and asked for an application form.

"Why Paraguay?" Peter Dyck asked.

"Some of my relatives are going there."

"Are you unhappy here?"

"No, not at all," I answered quickly. "I'm very satisfied."

"Then wait a little longer," he smiled. "Paraguay is no place for a widow with four small children." Briefly, he outlined the dangers and hardships of pioneering in a wilderness. "Canada is a much better place for you to begin a new life," he said.

"But I have no sponsor."

"We haven't tried everything yet," he said kindly.

Meanwhile, Canada approved the immigration application of my mother and Annie, and Isaac's mother and sister. Soon they were sent to a transit camp in Gronau. In June 1949, they left for Canada with a promise that they would try hard to find us a sponsor. My sister Tina joined her new German husband in another town. Tante Anna had left for

Paraguay in October 1948. Once more I was being separated from my family.

The children and I also moved from one refugee camp to another—from Sulzbach to Backnang, from Backnang to Gronau, from Gronau to Eppe, from Eppe to Fallingbostel. Clearly, there was no permanency for us in Germany.

Canada Has Accepted Us

One day, Isaac's mother wrote me from Kitchener, Ontario, Canada, that her cousin, John Tschetter, in Manitoba had agreed to sponsor us. Overjoyed, I filled out another application for Canada, and this time we were accepted. I wanted to celebrate this momentous event, so I bought some candy and distributed it among the children in the refugee camp. At the same time, my cousin and his family also received acceptance for Canada, but he didn't share in my celebration. "How will you support yourself?" he worried. "I expect to be working for a Canadian farmer, but what will you do?" His pessimism dampened my excitement and filled me with unsettling doubts. The last thing I wanted was to be a burden on my relatives in Canada. With God's help, I would work hard, I promised myself. Our sponsors would not be sorry for helping us.

Those of us accepted by Canada, thirteen persons in all (including my cousin and his family), were told to wait for a ship which would be leaving from the German port of Bremerhaven. Instead, a notice arrived that we would be going on an Italian freighter leaving from Naples, Italy. Quickly, we packed our things and took a train going over the Alps and through the Brenner pass into Italy. As I listened to the clacking of the train and saw the countryside whizz by, I remembered how often I had travelled with my children seeking a safe shelter. Then fear for our lives had

187

compelled us. Now in search of a new country, I felt the weight of uncertainty, but I also felt, for the first time, the thrill of adventure. When the train emerged from another very long tunnel, I caught a glimpse of the Mediterranean Sea glistening in the August sunshine. My heart leapt at this glorious sight.

The train stopped at the Naples train depot. Immediately, numerous street urchins pressed against the windows and doors asking for a handout. The police chased them away, but the children clambered underneath the train cars, and emerged on the other side, banging on the windows and calling to passengers for alms. The whole station was crowded with people shoving and shouting, reminiscent of refugees fleeing in a war, but this was a country at peace. *How strange,* I thought.

Soon a truck took the thirteen of us to the International Refugee Organization (IRO) Emigration Transit Camp Tirpitz. A fence six feet high encircled this former military base. As the truck approached, an iron gate opened for us and we entered a cobblestone yard and approached a three-storey building. I noticed how the gates banged shut behind us. I was keen on exploring an Italian city, but during our two-week stay at this camp, the gates remained closed. *So much for sightseeing,* I thought. The camp was filled with people of many ethnic backgrounds–Jews, Russians, Poles and Germans—all waiting to immigrate, some to Palestine, some to Australia, and some, like us, to Canada. A loud speaker blared out announcements continuously: "All women report to the kitchen for duty," and many other instructions. Soon I was peeling potatoes and helping with meal preparation. Before I left our room on the third floor, though, I instructed my girls to watch our stuff against stealing. Upon our arrival, I'd been warned that everything that wasn't nailed down would walk away. I soon discovered that this was no exaggeration.

For one hour each morning, the washrooms were opened and everybody pushed in. The children and I were jostled in the crowd as we tried to get near a sink. Suddenly, I felt my towel being yanked off my shoulder. Of course, there was no telling who had taken it. But from then on, I had to make do with one towel for the entire family. I fetched our meals in a small army pot which was issued to me upon arrival. The children and I ate our meals outside while sitting on the grass under a tree. Placing the lid beside me, I passed the pot around for everyone to take a helping. After we'd finished eating, and Fred had scraped the pot clean with his finger, I rinsed it out under a tap. When I turned around, the lid was gone. I was sick with worry, for we had been told that we would not be allowed to leave the country unless we returned every item in good condition. I bartered for another army pot, using cigarettes; the substitute pot was older and dented but it still had a lid on it. Two weeks later, when we left the camp, a young camp worker grabbed my hard-earned pot and tossed it onto a pile. He didn't even check to see if it had a lid on it.

On August 20, 1949 we boarded the Charlton Sovereign, an Italian freighter heading for Halifax, Canada. Eager to see the sights, I spent every possible moment on deck. As our ship plowed the quiet, deep blue waters of the Mediterranean we passed some beautiful islands. Schools of giant fish and large turtles swam in the water. The ship passed through the Straits of Gibraltar and entered the turbulent, grey waters of the Atlantic Ocean. Now our freighter rolled and pitched with every wave. Many people, including my children, became seasick. Even some of the crew became ill. A loudspeaker announced that help was badly needed in the kitchen and elsewhere. I volunteered to clean the toilets. But there wasn't enough help on board and the ship became dirty. The food was badly prepared. Much of it was dumped into garbage cans beside the dining room door.

During the three weeks of the voyage, I never got seasick. I spent much of my time on deck gazing over the wide expanse of rolling water. In all directions, as far as the eye could see, water moved in restless motion. In the morning, the sun rose out of the ocean and in the evening it sank into the ocean. What an awesome sight! I couldn't get enough of it. Sometimes large schools of whales followed our ship. We also saw dolphin leaping into the air, then disappearing into the waves again. As a child, I had read about the ocean in my father's books. Now, for the first time, I was actually seeing it. Its grandeur went beyond anything I ever imagined.

On the morning of September 2, 1949, I awakened to the blaring of a fog horn. I hurried on deck and into a milky fog enveloping the ship and the ocean. When it finally cleared a day and a night later, the sun spilled over the waves, and there, not far away, we saw land. As we came closer, we saw the shoreline of Halifax, and then we were near enough to distinguish people walking along the shore. Canada at last!

Arthur Voth from Pennsylvania, U.S.A., who "discovered" the Loewen family
in Austria and was subsequently responsible for reuniting them
with members of their family and the Mennonite community. He worked
in Europe from 1946-1948 for MCC in the resettlement of war refugees

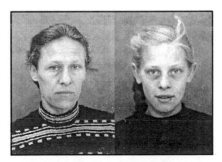

Passport photos. Left to right: Neta, Lena

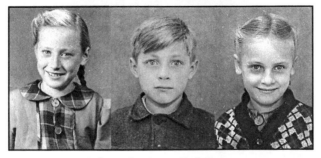

Left to right: Agnes, Fred, Katie

A group of refugees leaving Austria for an MCC camp in Germany, 1948. Neta (to the left of the Red Cross) with Lena, Agnes, Fred, and Katie (in the circle). Front row extreme right is Arthur Voth, MCC worker from the United States.

Annie, 19, as prisoner-of-war in Yugoslavia suffered from gun-shot wounds to both of her legs. Two years later she miraculously escaped across the border into Austria where she found her family again.

In Canada, Neta (middle) is joined by her mother, Anganetha Dyck (left),
who immigrated to Canada in 1948, and Tante Anna (right)
who immigrated to Canada from Paraguay in 1955.

Left to right: Katie, Tante Anna, Fred, Lena, Agnes, Neta

Left to right: Agnes, Katie, Lena

Henry, who survived many years in a Siberian labour camp,
visited his family in Canada 1976.
Left to right, Annie, Henry, Neta

Tina and Henry are reunited in Germany after
more than 40 years of separation

Neta with her eleven grandchildren, 1985
Front row, left to right: Anne-Marie, Becky, Heather, Suzie
Back row, left to right: Jonathan, Daniel, Esther, David, Elizabeth, Cathy, Peter

Neta with three great-grandchildren: Philip (on Tante Anna's lap),
Miriam (left), and Nathan (right)–Hallowe'en 1998

One of Neta's great loves was gardening and wherever we lived we had flowers
blooming either in a tin can on the table or in a small garden. "When life was tough,
I planted flowers," she said. "They always bloomed for me."

PART THREE

From Immigrant to Citizen of Canada (1949-1997)

CHAPTER THIRTEEN

Canada, So Rich
and Free!

THE CHARLTON SOVEREIGN docked in Halifax on September 3, 1949. Before we left the ship, I received one hundred dollars so I could buy food in our new country. After years of feeding the family with almost no resources, this seemed like an enormous amount. Katie had been ill the entire trip, and she was so weak, she could hardly walk. A man carried her up the gangplank and into the customs shed. Now that we were on solid ground again, I hoped Katie would be able to eat and become stronger.

At the customs shed my cousin surveyed my luggage with a doleful look. He pointed to a crate I had nailed shut, "How are you going to open *that* for inspection?"

I shrugged my shoulders.

"If you don't, Canada customs won't let you in."

Oh, no! I should have thought of that, I reproached myself. *Now what?*

A custom's officer came over and asked to see my passport. "And these are your children?" he asked pointing to Lena and Agnes standing beside the crate and Katie and Fred sitting on top of it.

"Yes."

He smiled, stamped my passport, then moved on. It all happened so quickly that it left me in a daze. Was this all there was to it? I stared at his back, wondering if, at any moment, he'd turn around and demand to see the contents of my luggage. But no, he busied himself with other immigrants. We were finished! Meanwhile, a woman came by and handed each of my children a booklet made of colourful construction paper. On each page was a picture cut out of a greeting card. Canadian children had made these booklets to welcome our children into Canada. Such a thing had never happened to us before. In the days ahead, I would continue to be amazed at the hospitality of Canadians.

My children and I boarded a train and were comfortably seated when my cousin and his family entered. I couldn't resist flashing him a triumphant smile. In the evening, our train left Halifax for Montreal. After a restless night, we entered Montreal's huge train station. The train to Winnipeg wouldn't be leaving until late afternoon, so we had a few hours to pass.

First, my cousin's wife and I went scouting for food. We found an ice cream shop and soon all thirteen of us were licking double-decker cones. How my children's eyes glowed at this delectable treat! Between all of us, we gave the ice cream man a lot of business.

We also found a small grocery store. As I entered, the sight of so much food took my breath away. I stared at the piles of bread, the fresh vegetables and fruit, the beautiful cuts of meat, the wonderful variety of dairy products, and the plentiful boxes and tins with bright labels. I had never seen so much food in one place before. Timidly, we watched as other shoppers collected their groceries. "Neta,

I think we're supposed to help ourselves," my cousin's wife whispered. We collected some groceries, then approached the cashier and handed her a wad of dollar bills with an explanation: "No English." She smiled and helped herself to the right amount. We carried our groceries to the group waiting at the depot. In no time, all the food was eaten, and we went back for more. I bought bananas, which I had never even seen before, and lots of peanuts. We were munching on something all day long and still we had money left over. (Food was cheap in those days.) "What a rich country!" we kept saying to each other.

Towards evening, the train left Montreal for western Canada. Because we didn't speak English, we wore a card around our necks with our destination written on it so the conductors could see at a glance where we were going. My cousin and his family were going to Winnipeg and I was going to Holmfield, Manitoba. Soon after leaving Montreal, I placed Lena and myself beside two windows on opposite sides of the train so we could read the signs. We didn't want to miss our stop. After a whole night and half a day of travelling, I became really worried. The topography had changed from pleasant farmland to enormous boulders, numerous lakes, and forests of stunted evergreen trees. *Alaska,* I thought with a start. *We've missed Canada and entered Alaska.* "Lena, ask the conductor if we've missed getting off at the right place," I called to my oldest.

"But Ma, I don't know how."

"You've studied English in school."

"Yes, I can say 'How are you? I am fine. Please give me a little chocolate. Good bye.'"

"Think hard," I said.

The conductor listened carefully to my daughter's question, then his face creased in a warm smile. He came over and placed his hand on my shoulder. "You're okay," he smiled. "Okay." He gestured to the card hanging around my neck and back to himself. I understood he would take full responsibility to make sure we got off at the right place.

The size of Canada continued to amaze me. If we'd been travelling in Europe, we'd have crossed several countries by now. Finally—after what seemed like a very long trip—we arrived in Winnipeg where most of our group were picked up by their sponsors. The children and I spent a night in Winnipeg, and the following day we took a train to Brandon. I had no idea how far that was. How would I know where to get off ? I couldn't ask anyone.

At one place, two women got onto the train and took a seat behind me. To my delight, I heard them speaking platt deutsch. *They will help me,* I thought. Suddenly, they switched to English. Then they moved to the back of the car as far away from us as possible. *Are they ashamed of us?* True, we looked like immigrants, but we were Mennonites just like they were. I wanted to tell them, but then I remembered the incident on the train when a man from my home town had claimed half of the freight car for himself and his family. These women might not be interested in helping us either. Wounded pride kept me in my seat.

Holmfield, Manitoba

Towards 5 p.m., the train slowed and a conductor motioned for us to get off. *Here?* I thought. *In the middle of this wheat field?* I couldn't see a town. A tiny train station, a grain elevator, and half a dozen houses floated in a sea of waving wheat. Where was the town?

The children and I stood on the platform waiting for someone to pick us up, but nobody came. Two men moved boxes and crates across a platform. One of them approached me and said something in English. I shook my head, "*Kann nichts verstehen*" (I don't understand.) I took my address card off my neck and handed it to him.

His face brightened, "Ah, John Tschetter!" Grinning, he mimicked cranking a telephone and speaking into it. I smiled back and nodded.

Soon a red Ford arrived driven by a young woman. An older woman sat beside her.

"Liese and Sara Tschetter," they introduced themselves. Sara apologized profusely for not being at the station to pick us up. They had come looking for us the day before, and not finding us, they didn't know when we would arrive.

"How about some ice cream?" she asked my children.

The children's eyes sparkled.

After devouring the treat, we piled into the Tschetter's car. As the car rolled through large wheat fields, ears tinged golden by the sinking sun, I kept looking for signs of a village. Instead, the car stopped at a small house beside a huge barn. *How strange, I thought. Back in Ukraine our houses were bigger than our barns.* Sara had told me they had five grown children, one married and living on his own farm, but the rest still living at home with them. *Such a small house for so many people? I thought. How can they accommodate another family?* Liese showed us to our room in a closed-in veranda.

Soon Uncle John came in, dusty and tired from a day's work in the field. His greeting was so warm and friendly, that I liked him instantly. We gathered around a table laden with bowls of steaming mashed potatoes, hamburger patties in mushroom gravy, and an assortment of vegetable dishes.

"Help yourself," Sara invited. My children dug in with such vigour, I felt ashamed. Once we were alone in our room, I lectured them, "Take small helpings so there's enough for everyone."

The following morning I rose early to help with the milking. "You don't have to do chores," Sara said. "My boys will get lazy if you do the work."

But I couldn't resist. *I have to earn my keep*, I thought. And still my children ate like field hands. Before going to the table, I would say to my children, "When I kick you under the table I want you to stop eating. Understand?"

" Mama, you said in Canada we could eat until we're full," Fred's eyes mirrored confusion. "Why don't you want us to eat?"

"There isn't enough for everyone if you eat like that."

One day, Uncle John scanned the meagre portions his wife had placed on the table and shook his head. "Cook more food, Sara," he said.

"I don't want to upset the children," she said. "Their stomachs aren't used to it." During the six weeks we stayed with them, Sara cooked wonderful food, but there wasn't enough of it. We would have been grateful just to eat more potatoes or another slice of bread, but, of course, I didn't feel free to ask for more. She was often short with the children and I tried to keep them out of her way. Her curt remarks and her frequent sighing made me feel like we were a burden on this family.

On Sunday, the Tschetters took us to church. As I left the small church building, a woman said to me, "You're so lucky to be in Canada. You must be very happy."

A lump formed in my throat and I couldn't say a word. I walked past her not wanting her to see my tears. Never before had I felt so useless. I'd gladly have done any job the Tschetters had asked me to do, but Sara made it obvious they didn't want my help. I felt certain she wished we had never come. Much later, I found out the reason for Sara's aloofness. Isaac's mother had written them that if they would sponsor us, she would look after our room and board. But shortly before our arrival in Canada, she had backed out. Now the Tschetters were stuck with us.

One Sunday afternoon, Sara took Katie and me to visit some friends of theirs. Our hostess asked me many questions about the war, how we managed to escape, and what life was like as a refugee in Europe. Usually I had no trouble talking about our experiences, but I was so discouraged, I could hardly converse. Suddenly, I smelled the delicious aroma of coffee made with real coffee beans–not the roasted grain served in Ukraine or European refugee camps. It had been twenty years since I'd savoured the smell of *real* coffee—that was before the communists took everything away from us. The delectable smell and the promise of coffee revived me so completely that I began to answer our hostess' questions with my usual animation.

In a short while, our hostess served a delicious meal and placed a steaming mug of coffee before me, inviting me to help myself to cream and sugar. As usual, Katie dug into the food with gusto, much to our hostess' pleasure. She kept piling more food onto my daughter's plate which she happily devoured.

"She'll get sick," Sara cautioned. "She shouldn't have any more."

But our hostess' eyes twinkled with amusement. "What do you say, Neta?"

"Let her eat," I said. *She's been hungry for too long,* I thought. Besides, I could sense Mrs. Neufeld's genuine hospitality. I think Katie ate half a cake and drank five cups of coffee before she stopped, wiped the perspiration off her face, and grinned at the hostess. Back at home, she bragged to her siblings about the wonderful meal she had enjoyed. Fred's eyes grew round and wistful.

"Why didn't you take me along?"he asked.

After supper one day, I saw guests coming to the Tschetter's home carrying gift-wrapped parcels. *Must be somebody's birthday.* I hurried my children into our room and gave them strict orders to stay there for the rest of the evening."We will not interfere with their party," I said.

A knock on the door surprised me. "Neta, you and your children must come into the living room," Aunt Sara said. "We've made a shower for you."

What's a shower? I stared at her in confusion.

"Come, all of you," she insisted. "This is a welcome party for you."

A welcome party. Why would they do that for me, a total stranger? I felt very shy and awkward as I entered a room full of smiling people mostly from the Tschetter's church. My children filed into the room and sat quietly beside me. We received a beautiful blanket and some clothing items for each child.

Later, in the privacy of our room, as the children tried on their new clothes, Lena babbled excitedly. "It's not Christmas, it's not anybody's birthday, and still we get presents. Canada is a very good country." But I felt even more beholden to these kind people. I couldn't rely on people's generosity alone, nor did I want to. I longed for gainful employment and independence. We needed to make our own way and support ourselves. Not until this was in place, could I make a new life for us.

October days were crisp and cold. Sara provided extra blankets and a small electric heater against the chill in our room on the veranda. One night as I lay in my bed, I overheard a muffled conversation between John and Sara coming from the other side of the wall.

"Sara, they can't stay there all winter. They'll freeze to death."

His wife shot back, "You're against splitting up the family, so what else can I do?" I had never been one for eavesdropping, but now I snapped to attention. *Splitting up the family?* My heart pounded wildly and I strained to hear every word. Sara began reading a letter from Isaac's mother: "I will take Lena and Agnes...perhaps your son can host Fred...maybe you wouldn't mind keeping Neta and Katie?"

After a pause, Uncle John cleared his throat and said, "Well, Sara, if it's only for the winter, maybe we should consider it."

I was shocked. I had managed to keep my family together throughout all the years of fleeing, during the lean post-war years, and in the refugee camps. Here in this great, free country of Canada with its marvellous resources, my family was to be split up and scattered in three directions? I felt sick. But what could I do to stop it? What could I do to keep my children with me? I worried all night without coming any closer to a resolution, falling asleep near morning.

The next few days, my mind worked endlessly on the problem. If I had a job then I could rent a place somewhere else, but John and Sara knew of nobody who would hire me. Late one night, as I sat in our room feeling that our situation was hopeless, a strange light danced across the sky in yellow, green, and red ribbons. As I watched this awesome display of the northern lights, it reminded me of another time, five years ago, when God had come to me in a dream. Now, I heard him whispering comfort to me again, "Don't be afraid. The God who created these wonderful lights will make a way for you."

Although I was no closer to a resolution, I felt comforted.

A few days later, I received a letter from my youngest sister Annie. That was the best day of my life for it gave me the answer I was looking for.

> *Dear Neta,*
>
> *In a recent Bote* (Mennonite newspaper) *we read about your arrival in Halifax on September 3, 1949. I want to let you know Mama and I are in British Columbia living with Tante Helena Thiessen. Mama has been here for 3 weeks already; I came just one day ago. Our trip across the ocean on the Scythia went well. Mama wasn't seasick at all and I was only slightly ill. At first we lived at a farmer's house in Manitoba, but he had no work for us, so I went to Winnipeg and found a house cleaning job. On August 28 Tante Helena came from B.C. to get us. Mama went immediately , but my employer insisted I stay another month. That's why I came so much later. Tante Helena has a vegetable farm which she manages with her two bachelor sons, John and Peter. Henry, her oldest son, has a chicken farm and a large house. I work as a fieldhand and earn 40 cents an hour. The work is not hard. Lena and Agnes could do it. The climate is much milder here than in Manitoba. In fact, today I weeded carrots. Next week we'll be harvesting potatoes. British Columbia is very beautiful. The country reminds me of Austria.*
>
> *If you don't like Manitoba or you don't have work there, please write us. Tante Helena said you can come here if you want. The Thiessen boys will pay for your trip."*

I was jubilant. What an answer to prayer! I sent a reply with the next outgoing mail. "Yes, I want to come." The

Tschetters, of course, were delighted with this new turn of events.

Soon Annie's reply followed with further instructions.

Dear Neta and Children,

I'm thrilled you are coming to B.C. Please write us immediately to tell us the children's exact ages and when you plan to leave and from where. As soon as we have this information, the Thiessen boys will wire you the tickets. It takes only three hours for this transaction. Your destination in B.C. is New Westminster. We'll be at the train station to pick you up.

Take bread, butter, cheese and fruit for the journey. Don't be skimpy, take enough so you won't be hungry. I know you're worried about your Reiseschuld, (travel debt to the sponsors) *but don't worry, Neta. After I've paid off Mama's and my debt, I'll help you pay yours.*

Tante Helena is looking forward to meeting you all. She loves to sing and I told her how beautifully you and your girls sing together. At first Tante can offer you just one room, but eventually, you'll get more space she said. So please come. I know you'll like it here. If you come soon, you can help in the potato harvest.

Train Ride To British Columbia

It didn't take me long to pack. The next day, on a crisp October morning in 1949, John Tschetter drove us to the CPR train station in Brandon. He went to the wicket to pick up our tickets.

"No tickets under that name," the clerk said.

"But they must be here. They were wired yesterday from British Columbia."

The clerk looked through all her files. "I'm sorry," she shrugged. "The tickets aren't here."

"What do I do with you now?" Uncle John looked totally frustrated.

"Please pay for our tickets," I said. "I'll reimburse you as soon as I can."

John Tschetter paid, then helped us onto the train. Soon we were on our way west. (The tickets cost about $70 since Fred and Katie travelled half-fare.)

I had no idea Canada was so big. All day we travelled through flat prairie. The next morning, we entered the Rocky Mountains in Alberta. For hours I gazed at the craggy, snow-capped mountain peaks on either side of the train. Annie was right, the country did resemble the Austrian Alps. As we snaked through narrow valleys, I thought, I *hope they don't live here. Those mountains would suffocate me.* I heaved a sigh of relief when the train entered wider stretches of orchards, but the hills surrounding the orchards, were so barren. And then, to my dismay, the train began to snake through mountains again. Where were the rich farm lands Annie wrote about? Finally, the train left the mountains and entered acres of fields and pasture lands with a backdrop of snow-capped mountains.

"Mission," the conductor said. "This is where you get off."

As I stood on the platform with my children, I looked for a familiar face to welcome us. All around us people were greeting each other and driving away, but nobody came for us. *They'll be here soon*, I kept telling myself, but an hour later, still nobody. Eventually, the station master called a taxi for me. I handed the address of our relatives in Surrey to the driver, and soon we were on our way. We drove across a bridge spanning the Fraser River (it reminded me of our Dnieper at home in Ukraine), and into the beautiful farmland of the Fraser Valley. The trip to Surrey seemed endless, and I became increasingly convinced that everything in Canada was far away. At last, the taxi stopped at a house on Mud Bay Road. The driver hopped out and unloaded our baggage. He held up one hand showing five. I handed him a five dollar bill; he nodded, then drove off.

I stood beside the road and surveyed the modest farm house, hoping that at any moment Annie and Mother would come out, but nobody came. Only a big dog roamed the farmyard. *Is this the right place?* I walked closer to the house and peered through the living room window. Nobody was at home. But it must be the right place, for it coincided with the address on my card. So we sat down beside the road and waited.

Finally, a large Chevrolet pulled up onto the driveway. Annie and my mother hopped out. "Neta! Children!" My mother shouted, "How did you get here?"

"We've just come from the train station," Annie added.

"But I didn't see you there," I said.

Later, while eating lunch, we were still trying to figure out how we could have missed one another. "Where did you get off?" John Thiessen asked again.

"I think the place is called Mission," I said.

"Mission!" he exclaimed. "But you were supposed to get off in New Westminster."

After much noisy chatter, the mystery of the missing tickets and the mix-up in destination was solved. We had taken the CPR train from Brandon to Mission, B.C., whereas our tickets had been wired to the CNR station in Brandon which stops in New Westminster, B.C.

In the end, everything worked out fine. The Thiessens got a refund and I saved enough money that fall to pay back John Tschetter.

CHAPTER FOURTEEN

Our Home
in Surrey, B.C.

IN THE AFTERNOON, I joined the harvesting crew on the potato field behind the Thiessen's house. The sun warmed my back as I dug my hands into the soft, black earth, and collected beautiful potatoes into a pail. In the field I met Mennonite people from Aldergrove and Clearbrook who spoke platt deutsch. *This feels like home,* I thought, *I will be happy here.*

Tante Helena, my grandmother's sister, had three bachelor sons: Henry, Peter, and John and one daughter, Nettie. All three men lived with their mother and slept in one bedroom upstairs and Nettie and her family lived right next door. Annie and my mother shared the second bedroom upstairs. As the children and I were shown to our bedroom downstairs, Tante Helena said, "Soon Henry's renters will be leaving and then you will be moving into his house." True to her word, a few days later, I saw people moving out of Henry's small farm house. But I felt uneasy. Had they been kicked out on my behalf? I ran over to talk to the woman and to my delight she spoke German. "You needn't move out." I said. "We could share one house, don't you think?"

She looked at me rather puzzled.

"I'm used to sharing space," I smiled. "In the refugee camps, three families sometimes lived in one room."

"Thank you," the woman said, looking slightly amused, "but in Canada we do things differently." She walked into the house to retrieve another box and carried on with her moving.

Soon the children and I moved into Henry's two bedroom farmhouse with a huge veranda.

My girls waltzed from room to room.

"Is all this for us?" Lena exclaimed. "How can we live in so many rooms all at once?"

"Our very own kitchen!" Agnes exulted.

"Look at this huge bath tub," Fred said. "All of us can fit into it at the same time!"

To pay for our rent, we looked after Henry's chicken farm and potato crop. Mornings and evenings my girls gathered eggs, cleaned and graded them, and put them into flats. Meanwhile, I worked in the Thiessen fields with Annie and my mother harvesting potatoes. What a pleasure to hurry to the field scattered with beautiful netted gems, grab a bucket and fill it. The days were sunny and warm. Often as I looked over at my loved ones happily filling their buckets, my heart almost burst with gratitude. My family was intact and I was earning our own keep. At fifty cents an hour, by the end of the harvest, I had saved enough money to repay our entire travel debt to British Columbia, and I still had money left over. I also had several house cleaning jobs lined up for the winter.

My children attended Kensington Prairie Elementary School on Brown Road, a small country school a mile and a half away. I worried how the children would manage in school not knowing English. Those were the days before English-as-a-second-language classes. The teachers merely lumped the youngest three into grade one. Katie, who was now six years old, was in her right element, but Agnes and Fred felt out of place. Lena, who was exceptionally tall for her age, was placed into grade three with kids half her size. Like her siblings, she spent most of class time colouring pictures. On that first day at school, my girls looked like traditional European school girls with their long, thick braids, an apron over a cotton dress, thick woolen stockings and laced leather shoes. For awhile I insisted on "proper dress" (including stockings and aprons), but when I found out that Agnes and Lena were rolling down their stockings and taking off their aprons just out of sight of the house, I gave up the battle. Soon my children dressed like their Canadian schoolmates. But there were many other cultural differences. Fred had never even held a baseball bat before, let alone hit a ball. He'd never dribbled a basket ball or shot a basket. My children didn't know the songs, the stories, the comics, and the movies their peers had grown up with, nor the holidays. Take, for instance, the Hallowe'en Party at school, with its masked and costumed people, apple dunking and dart throwing...it was all so strange. Our neighbour's children sometimes brought over comic books but my children didn't understand them at all.

Henry, who'd come to Canada in 1920, seemed to get pleasure out of mocking us as we struggled with English. Had I known then that Henry's English was quite deplorable, I might have come up with a comical reply. But back then, he was "the expert" and our landlord, so his words carried weight. One morning, he sat by our kitchen table, a sweat- rimmed hat pulled deep over his small head. Blue smoke circled his sallow face as he puffed on a cigarette. "Too bad about your kids," he said.

I stopped peeling potatoes. "What about my children?"

"They're not normal," he said.

"What do you mean 'not normal'?"

"They no laugh at funnies in papers," he let out another long puff of smoke. "They no can read English words. Now when we came to Canada—"

"You could speak English in three weeks," I finished for him.

"Right. " He smirked. "Your kids retarded, that's why—"

I could feel my cheeks flush.

"You no can see that," he grimaced. "You're their mother. Nettie and I—"

An uncontrollable rage propelled me forward. I flung open the door and shouted, "Out! Get out." Though he was larger and heavier than I, I grabbed him by his sweaty shirt collar, yanked him forward, and threw him out the door. His seat thump-thumped on every step, then it hit the ground kicking up swirls of dust. He picked himself up and shuffled to his mother's house. I leaned against the door-jamb trying to get control of myself. Immediately, remorse set in. What had I done? That detestable little man was our landlord, after all. No doubt, he would tell the rest of the family about my fit of anger. My mother and Annie would be so ashamed of me. And Tante Helena? No telling what she would do.

I didn't see Henry for the rest of that day. Normally, he would be harassing the children as they cleaned eggs, or he would poke his head in after supper to remind me that our pile of wood was getting low or some such thing. But not today. Nor the next day.

Now what? I thought. *He'll throw us out and we'll have nowhere to go.* For the hundredth time, I wished I would have considered the source of that rude comment and controlled my temper.

On the third day, as I saw Henry shuffling up our driveway, I set the table for coffee and mentally rehearsed my apology. But I didn't have time to give one. He burst through the door, fixed his beady eyes on me, and laughed uproariously.

"Your mother say you no get mad," he said, "but I show her." He laughed so hard he had to hold onto the table. "You get mad all right."

That day, I thanked God for Henry's sense of humour, however strange it was.

Soon Henry moved into the house with us and occupied the second bedroom. Apparently, that was also part of the rent bargain. Now I had to control my temper on a daily basis. My girls and I shared one bedroom, sleeping two persons in a bed, while Fred slept on a cot in the room that had a bathtub; no toilet, though, for we used an outhouse. Being under Henry's constant scrutiny presented a challenge for my children as well. Often I had to tell them, "Never mind what he says. Be nice anyway."

The winter of 1950 was cold and the cookstove was our only source of heat. The wood was so wet that I had to dry it in the oven before we could burn it. Our house was often dark, for Henry did not allow more than one light bulb in use at a time. He often grumbled about the amount of water I was using. But despite his idiosyncrasies, he did help me get established in our new country. Sometimes, he brought me a chicken from the barn for our supper. He told me I could help myself to all the cracked eggs and potatoes I wanted. During hunting season, he'd sometimes bring me a pheasant.

The children learned English quickly. By the end of that first year, all of them were in their proper grades: Lena in grade seven, Agnes, in grade five, Fred, in grade three, and Katie, in grade one.

Work On The Kennedy Farm

The following May, I began to work as a fieldhand on Matt Kennedy's farm. All day, I pushed a wheelhoe up and down the long rows of carrots just peeking through the ground. I had no watch, of course, but at noon, the foreman let me know it was lunch time. I gulped down my sandwich, then resumed the wheelhoeing. A wheelhoe resembled a miniature plow. You pulled back on the handles then pushed forward hard, slicing the earth with two blades thus dislodging the weeds between the rows. For eight hours, I made the same motions: pull back, push forward. By quitting time, all my muscles ached. Seeing me limp into the yard, Henry laughed.

"You think life be easy in Canada," he taunted. "Just wait, worse times ahead."

Careful, I said to myself. *Control yourself.* I hobbled around the chicken barn away from Henry's taunting and burst into tears.

The next morning, I was pleased to see two other women at work. They smiled and began to talk to me. I shrugged my shoulders and lifted my hands in a helpless gesture: "No English." No matter, one woman continued to chatter in a friendly way. She pointed to my house dress, and shook her head. "No good." Then she slapped her pants and said "Good." That day our job was pulling weeds. The women crawled up and down the rows on their knees, whereas I bent over and my back got very sore. I could see how wearing pants was definitely an advantage; I would ask Henry for a pair of his castaways.

Throughout the day, the women tried to pull me into the conversation, but all I could do was shrug my shoulders. With enormous patience, Mrs. Witt and Mrs. Galaway set out to teach me English. No matter how funny my pronunciation of the words, they never laughed at me. I took note of this pleasant difference between Canadian and European culture. In all things, I found Canadians more tolerant than Europeans. In the summer months and on Saturdays or holidays during the school year, Lena and Agnes also worked in Kennedy's vegetable fields and gave their money to me. Matt Kennedy invited us to take home any culls (produce he couldn't sell). So for many months of the year I did not have to buy potatoes, carrots, lettuce, onions, or cabbage. This greatly reduced our grocery bill. In the winter, I did housework for the Kennedy family. Little by little my savings grew. Two years later, I paid off our travel debt to Canada. What a relief!

"I didn't expect you to pay back so quickly," John Tschetter wrote. "You even paid an extra 60 cents." In another three years—saving every penny that I and my children earned—I had saved $4,000 and was able to pay cash for our first home.

The Kensington Prairie Sunday School

The first time I joined the field hands to work on a Sunday was during the potato harvest. But soon, I realized that in Canada, Sunday was treated like any other day, harvest or no harvest.

For seven days a week, tractors hummed and people worked on the fields. In fact, making money seemed to take preference over going to church. Not wanting my children to grow up totally unchurched, I walked with them on some Sundays to a church in Cloverdale, a distance of six kilometres.

In the summer of 1950, two young ladies stopped at our house to invite my children to a Daily Vacation Bible School held in the Kensington Prairie Hall near us. I had never heard of such a club, but if it had to do with Bible teaching, I was all for it. I had been worried that my children were receiving so little religious training. I gave my consent and all but Lena attended; she was needed to work in the fields. When DVBS ended two weeks later, Mr. and Mrs. Burchart, farmers in the area , extended an invitation to a young couple in Langley to open a Sunday school in the community hall. Jim and Arwilda McGladdery accepted the invitation. With their seven children, the Burchart's four, and my four they were assured of at least one good class. But soon many more children came from the farming community and the group was divided into several classes, Lena being asked to teach one class.

Saturday night, the hall on the corner of Mud Bay Road and Coast Meridian Road was often used for a local dance. Sunday mornings, my children would help Jim McGladdery collect beer bottles, shove the benches into place, and distribute hymn books. At starting time, Arwilda, a small woman wearing a thin braid wrapped around her head, placed her baby on the lap of her oldest daughter, walked up front, and began to play a piano—an old upright Weber with cracked varnish and missing keys. Still, the music coming out of it was wonderful, we thought. Her husband would announce the number of a hymn and begin to sing loudly in his baritone voice. Soon everyone was singing along. In this little Sunday school organized by two untrained people, my children learned how to have a personal relationship with God. They experienced love and acceptance at a time when so much in their lives felt strange and unfamiliar. The Sunday school grew into a Sunday morning worship service and a mid-week Bible study. Sometimes, I joined them. Although the services were conducted in English and I understood very little of what was said, I followed along in my German Bible. In this wonderful fellowship of believers, I met several families who became my close friends to the present day. The Youth Group on a Friday-night became a highlight for my teens. On many occasions, Jim McGladdery packed his dilapidated van with wall-to-wall young people (no seat belts required in those days) and took them to a special youth rally being held either in Vancouver, Langley, or White Rock. My children looked forward to these outings.

When the McGladderies moved into our area, we were delighted. Many a Sunday afternoon, Lena and Agnes went to visit them. I'm afraid they may have disturbed their afternoon naps, but the girls were always made to feel welcome. And if they stayed until supper time, Arwilda simply put two more plates on the table and invited them to join them.

My girls' involvement with church did not go unnoticed by Henry. "Your girls, too damn religious," he'd grumble. "I say, girls not normal." Lena, 15, and Agnes, 13, ought to be dating boys and partying like other young people, he said. He did everything in his power to discourage them. He scolded and he mocked them. How incredible then, that some thirty years later, one lonely night Henry found God in a very personal way. "I cough up blood and I think I die," he said. "I cry to God to save me." He stopped for a moment searching for words. "I cannot tell you how, but He came to me," he said in a hushed tone. In the years that followed, Henry welcomed Bible reading and prayer. His favourite radio programs were *Back to the Bible* and *The Haven of Rest*.

Henry had experienced God's grace that is greater than all our sin.

CHAPTER FIFTEEN

A Home of Our Own

HAVING PAID OFF our travel debt, I began to save money for a house of our own. Mother and Annie had moved to Clearbrook, B.C. (which is now west Abbotsford) into their own little home on one acre. "Lots are being sold for $500," Annie wrote. "Hurry up and buy one."But I wanted a house with more acreage so I could keep a cow and some chickens and grow a vegetable garden. One day, a friend from Nieder-Chortitza told me of a house and three acres for sale in Yarrow, a Mennonite community about half an hour's drive east of Abbotsford. When I saw it, I knew that was what I was looking for. The day before I was to sign the papers, I told Mother and Annie that I would be moving to Yarrow.

"So far away?"my mother looked shocked. "We'll never see you then."

I noted the sadness in my mother's voice. In a flash, memories of those lonely years when I wandered from one refugee camp to another in search of my family crowded my mind. A terrible war separated us then and a miracle

223

of God brought us back together. My mother was right, none of us had a car and regular visits would be difficult. I would buy closer to my family. And so, I bought a city lot on Hillcrest Drive for $600 across the street from my mother's house. My mother's neighbour, a contractor, built a small, three-bedroom house without basement on it for $3,000. It was the exact amount I had saved up. Later, I learned that the contractor had wanted to help an immigrant family, so he had reduced his labour costs for me. We moved into our own little home in January 1955.

In the succeeding year, from early summer to late fall, I continued to work at Kennedy Farms. I boarded with friends in Surrey, leaving my three teens to fend for themselves all week long. (Lena had left home by then). Katie, 13, often begged me to stay home, and now in retrospect, I think I should have. But at the time, it seemed right to work for the Kennedys who, six years earlier, had given me a job as a new immigrant unable to speak English. Furthermore, my good friends—the first I'd made in Canada—were working there as well. On Saturdays after work, I caught a ride home with friends who owned a photo studio in Cloverdale but lived in Clearbrook. During the winter months when I was home in Clearbrook, I attended a small Mennonite church within easy walking distance of our house. Soon I made many wonderful friends there. I found a year-round job at Empress Foods, a food processing plant, and Clearbrook began to feel like home.

My Grown Children's Lives And Careers

After completing high school, Agnes worked in a bakery in Abbotsford. With our pooled resources, we soon bought a red Volkswagen beetle.

Every new purchase we made was a cause for rejoicing. Once Agnes brought home a two-slice pop-up toaster. Lena was ecstatic. "Wow! Are we ever rich!" she exclaimed. "We have a house, a fridge, a car, and even a toaster."

Lena completed highschool in Surrey, three years of study at the Briercrest Bible School, in Saskatchewan, then three years of nurses training at the Vancouver General Hospital. She married Bill Lescheid and the couple, with two small children, moved to Kenya, East Africa. After three-and-a-half years of missionary work with Africa Inland Mission, they returned to Canada where Bill taught high school and Lena worked as a nurse. They have five children: Esther, David, Elizabeth (born in Nairobi, Kenya), Catherine, and Jonathan. And now Esther, married to Geoffrey Beatty, has blessed me with three lively great-grandchildren: Miriam, Nathan, and Philip.

While Lena and Bill lived in Kenya, Agnes, Fred and Katie attended the University of British Columbia in Vancouver. Agnes often brought home guests from the university, and our little house on Hillcrest Road reverberated with laughter and good fun. Ours was a small house by most standards, but there was always plenty of room for friends.

After graduation from university, Agnes married professor Gary Ferngren in 1970. They moved to Corvallis, Oregon, where Gary teaches at the Oregon State University and Agnes has worked at various office jobs. They have three beautiful daughters: Suzie, Anne-Marie, and Heather.

Fred graduated from the University of British Columbia with a degree in engineering. He accepted a job with Atlas Steel in Welland, Ontario. Later, Fred and his first wife, Liz, who is a nurse, worked in Tanzania, East Africa, for two years. Back in Canada, Fred returned to U.B.C. to become a highschool teacher. The couple adopted three children: Danny, Peter and Becky. Now Fred lives with his second wife, Carol, within easy walking distance to my house. He is still teaching highschool science in Langley, British Columbia, and often drops by after school for a cup of coffee or to mow the lawn. I usually fight him for that privilege, though, for at 87, I still like to mow my own lawn!

Katie became a first-grade teacher and later switched to teaching English-as-a-second-language to immigrant children. She enjoys reading, travelling and hiking and is very involved in her church. Katie lives in a beautiful condo in Vancouver and often comes to visit me.

When my children, grandchildren, and great- grand-children gather around my dining room table, laden with zwieback, cold cuts, pickles, cookies, and cakes, I stop to listen to their noisy, happy chatter. A lump rises in my throat. How good God has been to me! The famine of our earlier days has become a feast. Not one of God's promises has failed me.

I gaze up at the chandelier spilling light onto the heads of my beloved family, and I remember that wonderful light that burst from the dark winter sky one fear-filled night in Poland, and I hear again the whisper of God's promise to me: "Neta, you and your children are standing in the light of My presence. I will never leave you, nor forsake you." A promise for all time.

Anna's Story: A New House And a Best Friend

My mother's youngest sister Anna Penner was just eleven years older than I. She immigrated to South America, in October 1948 on the ship *Volendam* which docked in Buenos Aires, Argentina. She was among the first refugees who went to Paraguay directly from the ship. For the rest of the passengers a tent city had been set up in the harbor area as temporary accommodation. In Paraguay, Anna worked side by side in the bush with Mennonite men—refugees like herself from Russia. While the men were clearing land to build a settlement in the eastern part of Paraguay, Anna, well into middle-age, cooked meals over primitive fires and baked bread in a make-shift oven made from an anthill. At first, Anna scooped into rain puddles to make tea. Then she helped carry buckets of damp earth away from a well-digging site. Homes were built out of mud and straw. The walls and floors were mud, the roof was grass (which Anna helped to cut and weave together), the windows and doors were just openings covered with burlap that once had been MCC bales. They kept out dust and grasshoppers, but not snakes. Once when Anna came home to her little mud hut she found a huge cobra curled up on her bed. She called for help and the men came running with machetes in hand. Although the snake was removed from her house, Anna had a hard time sleeping that night.

Soon the women and children arrived from the holding camp in Buenos Aires. Now the colony Volendam (as it was christened) needed a school and a hospital. Every adult was asked to make a certain number of mud-bricks. In bare feet, Anna stomped on mud and made hundreds of bricks for the village effort. After eight years of pioneering in Paraguay, Anna was able to immigrate to Canada. By this time, I had become a Canadian citizen and was able to act as her sponsor. Anna found a job as a cook in the Menno Home in Abbotsford, a seniors care home about six kilometres from my home. On her days off, she frequently came to visit me. How I enjoyed her company! All that she had suffered had not dampened her joy of living. She had an irrepressible sense of humour and a gentleness that made her an easy companion. When she retired I wanted to invite her to live with me.

Realizing we would need more room then, I thought of having an addition built onto our small home, but Agnes advised me to buy a bigger house instead. The idea appealed to me.

One day, my mother and I were visiting a friend in Clearbrook when I noticed a neighbour peg a FOR SALE sign onto his lawn. It was an attractive house on a quiet street with a large yard. Immediately my interest was aroused.

"I'll have a look at the house," I told my mother as I rose to leave.

Soon Dyck, the owner, gave me a tour of their three bedroom, one bathroom home. In the dining room I saw a custom-made china cabinet that covered one entire wall, a feature I absolutely loved. I didn't need to see any more.

"How much are you asking?" I said.

"Thirteen thousand."

"Isn't it customary to dicker with the price a bit?" I asked.

"Sure," he smiled. "What will you give me?"

"Twelve thousand five hundred."

"It's a deal," he slapped his pant leg hard.

Later that evening, when I told Agnes about my wonderful purchase, she peppered me with questions: "What kind of heating does it have? What's the siding like? How's the roof? Does it have a fireplace?" To all her questions, I said, "I don't know."

"Good thing you didn't sign anything yet," she said. "I want to see it before you do."

Agnes liked the house as much as I did. It was a deal.

Two months later we moved into our house on Sunrise Crescent across from the Tabor Home in Clearbrook, British Columbia. Some friends supplied a truck and helped me move in.

In June1955, Tante Anna moved into our home. At the time of this writing we have been house companions for over 40 years, longer than either of us have lived with anybody else. We are each other's best friend. Both Anna and I love to cook and entertain. Often my sister Annie and husband, Karl, come to visit us from their home in Abbotsford. Other friends join us and before long, our conversations hearken back to our war experiences. Sometimes there are tears, but most often there is laughter as someone shares a humorous story. Often it's Tante Anna who'll share one of her most embarrassing moments with us. Once she told us about the time when she took her first taxi ride in Canada. That afternoon she and her friend Lydia had been to visit me. We'd had such a good time, that we hadn't noticed the growing darkness outside. When the women were ready to walk back to the Menno Home, I insisted on calling a taxi. "It's too dark for you to be out walking," I said.

The two women climbed into the backseat and the taxi got on its way. Suddenly the women heard a man's voice. The driver answered, and the men carried on a conversation.

"Who's he talking to?" Lydia whispered in her native German.

"I don't know,"Anna said. "But there's another man is in this car and they're up to no good!"

As the darkened countryside flitted by and nothing looked familiar anymore, the women became convinced that these men had evil intentions. Why else would one of them be crouching so low that he couldn't be seen?

"When he slows at a stop sign," Anna whispered, "be ready to jump."

Suddenly the car stopped. The driver got out and opened the passenger door.

"Here you are, ladies, safe and sound at the Menno Home," he said in perfect German.

"Later I learned about two-way radios," Anna laughed. "I also found out the taxi driver goes to my church. Imagine, I have to face him every Sunday!"

That was Anna. She saw humour in almost any situation. And she loved celebrations, especially birthday parties. For the entire month of February she celebrated her birthday. Every weekend she'd take another group of friends to Mama Panda—at her expense, of course. After filling up on Canadian and Chinese food, she invited all her guests home for dessert: a generous slice of German torte which she had baked the day before.

In June 2000, Anna fell and broke her hip. Lena called the ambulance and accompanied her great-aunt to the hospital. Despite the pain and the long wait in the emergency room, Anna was cheerful. She recounted some of the blessings of her life, foremost, the blessing of spending more than 45 years in our home. "How I wish Jesus would call me home," she told Lena. "My greatest fear is of becoming a burden to your mother." God granted Anna's wish: A month later she died at age 97.

My Brothers...and Isaac

You may be wondering about the rest of my family. My three brothers spent many years in Siberia in labour camps. While most of their colleagues perished, by God's grace, they survived. For many years they knew nothing of each other or their families' whereabouts. Eventually, through the Red Cross, they found each other again. In time, news of their family in Canada also reached them. Before my mother's death on October 3, 1982, she had the great pleasure of seeing two of her sons again. In the fall of

1979 Peter visited us in Canada and Henry followed two years later. Despite decades of separation from each other there was an immediate rapport: speech and mannerisms alluded to a family connection. Still, the harsh regime of communism had left its mark. My brothers couched their language in riddles as though they were afraid to speak openly. They were overwhelmed with the opulence of Canada: stocked shelves in the stores, roads choked with cars, electric lights burning everywhere even in empty buildings. When I informed Peter that we would be making a sightseeing trip to the interior of British Columbia he asked, "Don't you have to inform the police before we go?" When a proprietor wanted to give him a suit, Peter became alarmed. "Can he really do this? Doesn't he have to give an accounting to the authorities?" When we took Henry to the Canada/U.S.A. border in a rural country setting and pointed to the shallow ditch which divides the two countries, he was astonished. "That's it!" he exclaimed. "No watch towers, no machine guns, no military personnel..." Such freedom was foreign to him.

After years of waiting and much red tape initiated by my sister Tina in Germany, my brothers Gerhard, Peter, and Henry with their families immigrated to Germany. In May 1998, Annie and I travelled to Germany to meet Tina and our three brothers. What a reunion we had! There was so much catching up to do. After a separation of over forty years, where do you begin? We began by telling each other our stories–stories of great hardship, yes, but also stories of God's loving intervention. Often the narrator would end with the heartfelt words: "God has been good to me!"(You may read some of the stories in the appendix.)

I have not heard any news of Isaac. I admit, when other women found their husbands again—as it sometimes happened—hope stirred within me. Yet undoubtedly, Isaac died on that fateful night shortly before Christmas 1943. I am comforted to know that my husband is with the Father of heavenly lights who does not change like shifting shadows.

Epilogue
By Lena (October, 2008)

More Life To Live

MY MOTHER SAT precariously on a narrow examination table in the doctor's office, her blue hospital gown tied in the front. The surgeon examined a hard lump in her right breast, then he turned to me. "I strongly suspect cancer," he said. "I'll get her into hospital as soon as I can."

As a nurse, I had expected as much, and yet I had clung to the dim hope that since there was no history of cancer in our family, the tumour might not be malignant.

On the way home from the clinic, I carefully explained what the doctor had said: how a surgeon would do a biopsy first, and, if the tumour was malignant, he would operate.

"I don't want an operation," my mother said with finality.

"Then you will die."

She fixed her bright blue eyes on mine. "I'm ready to die," she said. "I've had a good life."

A good life? I wondered how she could say that after all the hardships she'd been through. I looked at this small, brave woman beside me and asked, "Mom, how did you do it?"

"Do what?" she asked.

"Live through all that turmoil—you know, losing your husband and home in the war, fleeing with four small children, starting over in a foreign country..."

"Lots of people were worse off than I," she said.

How typical of my mother! She quietly accepted whatever God sent her way. She never asked why me? As far as she was concerned, she'd had a good life.

"Are you tired of living?" I asked her.

Mother's cheeks flushed slightly. "My neighbour gave me some bulbs," she said. "She told me the flowers are very beautiful. I want to plant them and see for myself." *Yes, my mother always loved flowers*, I thought.

"You'd better have the operation then," I said quietly.

My mother agreed. A few days later, the surgeon performed a total mastectomy. I hurried to the hospital, wondering how I would comfort her. But when I arrived on her ward, she was not in her room.

"Where's my mother?" I asked the nurse.

"Probably gone exploring," she laughed. "We can't keep her in bed." I began searching the corridors for a small woman in a red house coat.

When I found her, she assured me she felt fine. But in her eyes, I detected her weariness and encouraged her to go back to bed. She snuggled under the blanket, then fixed her gaze upon me and said quietly, "I don't feel like a whole person anymore."

I winced at her humiliation. "Yes, I know," I said, trying to steady my voice. "But to me you're as beautiful as you always were."

As Mother's health improved, she began working in her garden again. She planted bulbs and geraniums and petunias and many other flowers, rejoicing in each one that graced her garden. She carried bouquets of flowers to her church or across the street to her friends in Tabor Home. Soon she was as busy as ever, entertaining company, helping out at church functions and sewing for her grandchildren. I relished our time together and our intimate chats.

Almost a year later, after a thorough examination, the cancer specialist said, "I find nothing to be worried about. You need not return unless your doctor finds something suspicious again." And for several years there was no need to return: Mother was in good health.

A Special Birthday Party

My mother hated any kind of public recognition. She did her good deeds in secret and then pretended she hadn't done anything at all. When she turned eighty, Katie, Fred, Agnes, and I tried to have a birthday party in her honor, but she absolutely refused to cooperate. But when her 90th birthday was drawing near, we were determined to celebrate in style. I managed to sneak her address book out of the house and began calling her friends. With each invitation I said, "We want to surprise Mother. Will you keep this an absolute secret, please." Her friends smiled and gave their solemn promise.

Finally, when all the plans were laid and it was too late to cancel, we decided to give Mom some warning. On that Sunday in June, Agnes told her that there would be a birthday party for her in the afternoon in the church basement. Many friends had agreed to come and there was no way she could back out now. Resigned, Mother put on her best royal blue dress, fussed with her hair, and dabbed a bit of lipstick on her lips. Timidly she entered the crowded guest room and took the seat I offered her beside me at the front. Soon more than a hundred guests had taken their places at tables decorated with white lace cloths, green place mats and bright marigolds.

Scanning the faces of the guests before me, I reflected how each had shared a slice of my mother's history: Some had grown up with her in Nieder-Chortitza; one woman had been present at her wedding to Isaac Loewen; Anna Harder had shared a room with her in a refugee camp in Poland. A little further back sat people who'd worked with her on Matt Kennedy's farms. Arwilda McGladdery, Dave and Gwen Thomas and Fred Burchart spoke of warm Christian fellowship enjoyed in Sunday school and Home Bible studies in Surrey. One person we did miss in this delightful company was Tante Anna; she'd died two years earlier at age 97.

My mother's blue eyes, which matched the lovely blue dress she was wearing, sparkled as she greeted her many friends. "And you're here, too!" she kept exclaiming. "How wonderful!" For many months, afterwards, Mother kept talking about her wonderful birthday party. "You must see my book," she said to guests who entered her home. Proudly she showed off the memory album of photos, poems, drawings and musings her grandchildren had made for her. One such entry follows.

A Grandson Remembers

Oma, as you look around this festive room of tables decorated with lace cloths, green mats, and bright marigolds, you will see many happy faces. Many people have come— some from great distances—to celebrate your 90th birthday. Why have we come? Because we want to tell you that you have enriched our lives in more ways than you realize. Let me share some of my fond memories with you now.

On a visit to your home, I remember your cheerful greetings at the door urging us to "Come on in." Then, seeing I didn't have a jacket on, you would hurry away to find a warm sweater and slippers for me to wear. "You must dress warmer," you'd chide me in a good-natured way.

I remember the amazing meals you made for us: the perogies filled with cottage cheese and doused with a rich sour cream sauce; the farmer sausage fried a golden brown, the tomato-cabbage borscht (the best I've tasted anywhere), the fruit mousse with lots of prunes in it, the *roll kuchen* eaten with watermelon, and the seemingly endless supply of buns, cookies, *platz* (like an open-faced pie) and cake. When we could eat no more, we would retire, happy and relaxed, to the living room to watch a Walt Disney movie on your television.

I remember the many Christmas gifts you made for me: rocket pajamas, knitted slippers, and a white lab coat which, as a medical doctor, I wear to my clinic with great pride.

I wonder what is the secret to living so well? Tell me, how does one stay healthy and happy for ninety years? Much of it is in God's hands, I know, but you've modeled for me some valuable life-lessons that I will strive to emulate.

You have remained physically active. At ninety years of age, you still live independently: you do your own cooking and cleaning, not only for yourself, but also for the many guests who pass through your doors. Besides, you look after your own yard and garden with its many plants and flowers. And you keep sweeping your driveway to clear it of pine needles–a never-ending battle. Your incredible physical stamina has been a source of inspiration for me and my patients.

You have remained mentally active reading many books of enduring quality, then telling us about them. You are keenly interested in world affairs–often you know more about current events than us younger people.

You have been socially active in your church, singing in the choir, serving in a ladies group, and working for the MCC Thrift Store, sorting clothing in their basement.

You live in the present moment. You never wallow in the *what ifs* of the past or pine for the *maybes* of the future. Your faith in God, coupled with a keen sense of humor, enables you to live each day to the full and to move on with courage and joy.

You enjoy the simple things of life. Your life isn't cluttered with fancy clothes, expensive jewelry or the latest technological toys. Your home has been a sanctuary where one can go to rest, to be fed, and to be strengthened in the bonds of family and friendship.

You've modeled for me what family is all about. Although your large family represents many nationalities and religions, you've treated us all alike. You've shown us how to put our differences aside and simply be family.

Oma, I'm almost two feet taller than you are, still, I look up to you with my deepest admiration. You have been a source of strength and inspiration to us all. Thank you for showing me how to live life with zest and courage.

Your loving grandson, David

(Dr. David Lescheid, BSc, PhD, ND from Ottawa, Ontario)

A Life Well Lived

When my mother approached her 91st year, the doctors diagnosed pancreatic cancer. The specialist said that considering her age, they would not be doing aggressive treatment.

So we took Mother back to her home from the hospital. I organized a 24/7 care plan with the help of my siblings and Home Care nurses. Some afternoons, when she felt a little better, I would take her for rides in the country.

Passing a meadow, she'd marvel at the bright yellow dandelions in the fields. When driving past a field of raspberry bushes, she'd remark on how neatly the vines had been tied in symmetrical arches. She'd even notice the color of a door or a roof and exclaim at its beauty. In her dying moments she found beauty in mundane detail, that I, in my busyness, scarcely noticed.

Mother had expressed a desire to see tulips before she died. So, on an afternoon, I took her to a tulip farm near Chilliwack, British Columbia. Steadying her thin frame on the open car door, a kerchief covering her snow-white hair, she gazed longingly at the rows of red and yellow, white and pink tulips undulating in the breeze. Was she thinking, *If this is so beautiful, what must heaven be like?*

Often she would quote a hymn that expressed her longing to be with Jesus, or her trust in Christ's death and resurrection for her salvation. Sometimes, after I had tucked her into bed, I would hear her singing in her now raspy voice hymns she had sung as a child with her father sitting in the twilight on a bench, leaning against the warm tiles of the oven, waiting for the kerosene lamps to be lit. She still knew the songs from memory.

Being certain of her heavenly home, my mother faced her death courageously. She spoke freely about it and made sure all her affairs were in order. Still, she was very much in charge of daily household duties, as well, making sure the lawn was cut, the house was tidy, and her many guests received a cup of tea and a cookie before they left.

One day she said, "If I had known that I would not have much longer to live, I would have baked more cookies."

When I laughed at this, she said, "No, seriously, I would have filled the deep freeze with cookies–you know the jam-filled ones the children are so fond of."

But in truth, her grandchildren were fond of their Oma. They flew in from all parts of Canada and U.S.A. to spend a few more hours with her. If possible, she'd struggle out of bed and sit with them at the kitchen table, an open photo album before her, and upon their coaxing, she'd tell them stories of her life.

"God has been good to me," she'd often say." Gazing at each of her grandchildren, she'd add, "He has blessed me beyond my imagining."

My mother died on May 17, 2003. Three years later, on March 24,2006 my sister Agnes also went to be with the Lord. Fred, Katie, and I have retired from our various professions. May we continue to live our lives in grateful dependence upon God–as Neta did.

Appendix I: Additional Stories

Angels Watching Over Me
by Tante Anna Penner

DURING THE WAR, I was a refugee in Yugoslavia. At the time I was living with other refugee women up the mountain near Ratkersburg. Partisan activity against German refugees made living there unsafe for us. So, when my sister in Germany invited me to come live with her, I found it very appealing. But first, I needed to obtain a visa. For that, I had to walk ten kilometres down the mountain to the train station, then take a train to Graz, Austria. If everything went well, I'd be home before dark.

On the appointed day, a friend joined me on the trip. As so often happens, the paper work took longer than anticipated, and we were late in boarding a return train to Ratkersburg. Daylight was fading fast, and then, sleet pelted the window. My friend got off at a station where her son lived, but I continued on the journey. I was the only passenger getting off in Ratkersburg. It was a stormy night and an icy wind tore at my threadbare coat. I hurried into the dimly lit station, sat down on a wooden bench, and deliberated what to do next.

To get back to the refugee camp up the mountain, I would have to walk alone in the darkness through the storm. I had no flashlight, and I would have to find my way up the narrow path through a forest where partisans might be hiding and then cross a dangerous mountain stream.

I'll spend the night here at the station, I thought, *and go home in the morning.*

A middle aged man busied himself behind the wicket. Timidly, I approached him: "Sir, could I spend the night here, please?"

"No, ma'am," he said emphatically.

"I have far to walk—" I began.

"Ma'am, I can't allow it," he said abruptly. He grabbed his coat and hat and fished for the keys in his pocket. Then he headed for the door.

At the door the man turned and said impatiently, "C'mon. I'm locking this place up." He added more kindly, "During an air raid, you'll be safer up the mountain anyway."

As I listened to the receding crunch of his boots on gravel, the knot of fear in my stomach tightened. "Father," I whispered, "I'm so scared. Take away this terror. Walk with me."

Suddenly a light fanned across the sky.

Oh, no, the bombers! I thought. Knowing that train stations are targeted, I moved away from the building. The light moved with me, clearly shining on my path.

I waited for the screeching of planes, then the explosion of bombs. Nothing. Instead, a deep quietness filled the countryside. An indescribable peace filled my heart, dispelling every trace of fear. The path lay bright at my feet. I began to hum a familiar hymn.

Then I realized the wind had stopped and the rain.

When I reached the swollen stream, I could clearly see the flat rocks sticking out of the foaming water. Surefooted I forded it.

The light guided and cheered me all the way up the mountain to the refugee camp. Two hours later, I knocked on the door. Someone yelled, "Who is it?"

"Anna Penner," I called back.

The door opened and a gust of wind grabbed it, almost tearing it off its hinges.

"Anna, come in," a woman called, pulling me inside."Such a terrible storm. Weren't you afraid?"

"No," I shook my head. "There was no storm where I was walking. Did it just start up?"

"No, it's been raging for hours."

Now I could hear it too: the howling wind, the sleet pelting the window panes, the moaning of the house.

"You must be soaked," a woman said. "Here, let me take your coat." I let her have it and she exclaimed in utter amazement, "Your coat is dry." She looked at me quizzically, then she said, "How could you walk through a storm like that and keep your coat dry?"

" There was no storm where I was walking," I said.

My friends looked at me curiously, much like they do now when I tell my story. How do I explain it? God sent His kindly angelic light to cover me and to guide me up the mountain. "Don't be afraid," was God's word to me, "for I am here." Yes, there have been times when I've been afraid, like when a snake wanted to share my home in Paraguay. Whenever I'm afraid, I sing a hymn like, "Oh, take my hand, my Father;" I recite a poem or a Scripture verse, and commit myself to God. He's always taken care of me and I know He will continue to do so.

So nimm denn meine Hande und führe mich	(Oh, take my hand, my Father, and lead me on)
Bis an mein selig Ende und ewiglich.	(Now and to my blessed end in eternity)
Ich kann allein night gehen, nicht einen Schritt;	(I cannot walk alone, not even one step)
Wo Du wirst geh'n und stehen, da nimm mich mit	(Wherever you are, take me with You)

Never Alone

by Annie Dyck

It was May 12, 1945, four days after the Second World War ended. A mass exodus of refugees and German soldiers plugged the village streets near Celje, Yugoslavia. Anxious to leave a communist country my mother, my sister Tina with her son Victor, and I joined the crowds of refugees trying to make their way into Austria.

Men and women, carrying all their worldly possessions in a burlap bag, pushed past others pulling wagons in which sat little children. Army trucks and jeeps, overflowing with German soldiers and civilians, were inching through the crowds. I hurried to keep up with my family. During our eighteen months of fleeing from Ukraine, we'd managed to stay together, and I wasn't about to be separated now.

The sun was shining, still there was a cool breeze. I buttoned the light maroon coat I was wearing over a blue cotton dress. My feet in summer sandals were cold for I had no socks. In the burlap sack I carried over my shoulder I had a blanket and a pillow. Since we'd been on the road for several days, we'd eaten all our food, but we hoped to get more once we arrived at a refugee camp in Klagenfurt, Austria. It wouldn't be long now, maybe by nightfall.

Victor, my seven-year-old nephew, took my hand. "Tante Annie, I'm so tired," he whispered. When I picked him up, his thin arms circled my neck and his cheek rested on my shoulder.

A blaring of horns made me move aside. An army truck was trying to pass. My mother, white hair spilling out of a kerchief, stepped forward, "Please, sir, take us along," she begged. "The child is tired."

"Get on then—in the back," the driver barked.

I squeezed my body beside a soldier sitting on the floor, feeling suddenly shy when I almost landed in his lap. By the grin on his face, I could tell he didn't mind sharing space with a nineteen-year old woman. The truck inched forward. Finally we arrived at the border.

To our dismay, partisan soldiers controlled the Yugoslavian/Austrian border. "Stop!" one shouted, pointing his machine gun into the crowd. People froze. Trucks came to a halt. "Everybody out," he ordered. After searching every piece of luggage, old women and children were allowed back on the trucks; young people, like myself and Tina, were ordered to step aside and join a group of people—mostly German soldiers. *What does this mean?* I wondered. *Why are they separating us from our families?* Suddenly I heard Mother shouting in platt deutsch from the back of the truck, "Tina, get back here. Your son needs you." Without the slightest hesitation, my sister hurried to her son's side.

Meanwhile, I wondered what would happen to me. I had a gut-feeling that this would not turn out well, especially when a partisan ordered us to march back into the village,

245

away from the Austrian border and freedom—and away from my family. In the crowd I recognized two girls from my home town: Maria and Helena Klassen. "Let's stay together," I whispered.

We marched for hours. Partisans on horseback, kept shouting, "Keep pace." Darkness fell. On a football field outside a village, we hunkered down for the night. I wrapped myself in my blanket and tried to sleep, but I couldn't stop shivering from the cold and the fright. What were they going to do with us?

Day after day we marched. An old man collapsed on the road. I watched with horror as a guard pointed his gun at him and fired, then kicked his writhing body into the ditch.

Try as she might, Maria couldn't keep up. A guard jammed his rifle butt into her belly. She fell to the ground. He kicked her, then walked away. One German soldier helped her up and whispered, "Girls, get into the middle." From then on a small brigade of seven German soldiers formed a shield around us and protected us. They also took care of us. When a strap on my flimsy sandal broke, a soldier handed me a pair of army boots. "Here, wear these," he said.

Day after day, the relentless march moved on. We had no idea where we were going. We had no food or water. When we came to a stream, we scooped up handfuls of water and lapped it up. We pulled up weeds along the road and chewed on them. One of the soldiers, a medic, filled his canteen with water and added a little sugar. Then he gave it to us girls to drink.

After eight days of marching, a man shouted, "Convoy, to the right." We moved aside to let a guard on horseback pass. He pulled in the reins and stopped his horse. "Damn Germans!" he shouted. He pointed his gun into the crowd and fired. A searing pain flashed through me. Blood spurted from my legs. I crumpled to the ground.

I knew I was hurt but I didn't find out how badly until later. (My left ankle was crushed and my right leg received five pieces of shrapnel.) Dimly I heard a man's voice say, "Anna, open your mouth." I swallowed some pills and sugar water. Then the medic wrapped tourniquets around my legs and bandaged them. He stayed with me until a Red Cross jeep arrived. Then he helped another medic lift me onto a stretcher. They covered me with a blanket and placed my burlap bag under my head. Because there was no room inside the jeep, my stretcher was placed on top of the jeep, and secured to the metal framework. I drifted in and out of consciousness. Once, I had the sensation that my burlap bag was falling, so I reached down, grabbed hold of it, and pulled hard. It wouldn't budge; so I pulled harder. I heard a voice from underneath me say, "Dear child, would you please let go of my head?" It turns out, there was a soldier sitting there and what I thought was my bag was actually his head.

The Red Cross jeep never made it to a hospital. Once more the partisans intercepted; they took possession of the jeep and ordered everybody to get out. As they placed my stretcher beside the road, one partisan asked me, "How did you get hurt?" I tried to tell him about the random shooting, but he cut me off. "You were trying to escape," he said. "Serves you right!" After that, when somebody asked me how I got my injuries, I said it was an accident.

The partisans gave orders for everyone to march on. Whoever failed to do so would be shot.

Most of the wounded soldiers shuffled on, but I couldn't walk; I couldn't even move my toes. The medic told the partisans that it was his duty to stay with the sick, but they wouldn't hear of it.

"Anna, I have to go now," he said sadly. "I'm not leaving you because I want to." His voice choked and he stopped to compose himself. "They've already warned me twice that if I don't go they will shoot me." Then he walked away. As I listened to his receding footsteps, it hit me hard: I was all alone in a hostile country.

Panic overwhelmed me, and I began to cry.

Would the partisans shoot me and discard my body like they had done with the old man?

"Jesus, help me," I cried, "I am so scared." Suddenly, I felt a warm Presence, like a mother hovering over a sick child. *"Don't be afraid,"* a Voice said. *"I am here; I will never leave you nor forsake you."*

"Then I am safe," I said softly. "Even if they shoot me, I will be okay." A deep peace enveloped me and I drifted off to sleep.

Early the next morning, I heard the rumble of wheels. I raised my head and saw two men in an oxen cart coming in my direction. Seeing me, one man jumped down and had a closer look. "My God! She's been shot," he said. "Come, help me lift this stretcher onto the cart." The men drove to a hospital in a village nearby. But an officer wouldn't allow me to enter. "We don't treat Germans here," he said. Instead, I was taken to the Communist Headquarters. There they lifted me off the stretcher and put me on a hard table. The pain from the jarring motion was excruciating and it took all my will power not to cry out. When they fired questions at me, I answered in Russian, surprising the interrogator.

"How come you speak Russian so well?" he asked.

"I was born in Ukraine and learned Russian in school."

"So you ran away," he said. "You figured the Germans would win this war."

"Yes," I said.

"Foolish girl," he sneered. "You could be at home in Russia eating white bread and look at you now." His lips curled into a smirk. "You think only the Germans are good."

"No, we had Russian neighbors back home and they were good people," I said. "There are good people and bad people in every race."

He was silent for a long moment. "You're right," he said. He picked up a pen and began writing on a paper. Then he handed it to me. "You may go to the hospital now," he said. "A prisoner-of-war camp is no place for you."

The hospital had no X-ray machines and very little equipment. A doctor (a German prisoner of war like myself) put a cast on my left leg to above my knee leaving a hole over the shattered ankle so the wound could be cleansed and dressed. He bandaged my right leg riddled with shrapnel. Then I was placed in a large open ward. Every bed was full. Catholic sisters in black habits moved about bringing food and water to the patients. During visiting hours, the room filled with friends and relatives. But nobody came to visit me. As I looked at the clusters of friendly people crowding around individual beds, I wanted to cry. If only I had one person who'd want to be my friend!

A month later, in June 1945, my cast was removed, and, even though my wounds were still infected, I was discharged from hospital and sent to a refugee camp near Maribur. It was a big school gym and we slept on the floor. I had no crutches, therefore, I couldn't walk. In the morning two young girls put their hands together to form a little chair and carried me outside to sit on the grass. In the evening they returned to carry me back into the building. At noon an old man brought me a bowl of soup.

Day after day, the same senseless existence. People with hunched shoulders and sad faces shuffled by. Few bothered to talk to me and I couldn't really blame them. By now the bandages, soaked with pus, stuck to my wounds and gave off a foul odor. My right leg was grossly swollen. Wild flesh grew from the wound in my left leg.

Feeling utterly helpless and forsaken, my life became unbearable. I wanted to die.

One day when the old man brought me my soup, I shook my head. "I'm not eating," I said. He tried to coax me, but I refused to take the soup. In a fit of helpless rage, he dumped the soup onto the ground and stomped of. In a short while he returned with a doctor. When he looked at my leg, he exclaimed, "Oh, my God! We've got to get you to a hospital."

The doctor lifted me up and put me on the front of his bicycle. Then he pedaled to the hospital. He promised to bring my belongings later which included my blanket, a pair of men's pants, and a pair of army boots with bullet holes in them; those were all my worldly goods.

At the hospital I was given a warm bath. After weeks of not having one, it felt so good. The bandages were removed and the doctor examined my wounds. "I don't know if we can save your left leg," he said. "We may have to amputate."

Imagine my relief, when the following day after surgery, I pulled the blanket back and discovered I still had both of my legs. The doctor had removed much dead tissue and a lot of pus, but my leg was spared!

Some weeks later, when the infection had cleared and my wounds had healed, I was discharged to a refugee camp where the same doctor who'd operated on my legs was the doctor in residence. He requested that I work for him in the sick bay and I was more than happy to do so. I made rounds with him, took temperatures, made up charts, gave out food and medications, held sick children on my lap, and even darned his socks and turned over his frayed shirt collars.

At first I was allowed the use of crutches, then I graduated to a cane. The day came when the doctor said, "It's time for you to walk unaided." As he saw me limping, he said, "walk on your toes, Annie, or you'll always walk with a limp." To do so was very painful, but I'll be forever grateful for the doctor's strict discipline. Today I do not walk with a limp.

One day a Russian Commissar came to visit the hospital. "I've come to tell you that you'll be going home to Russia tomorrow," he said.

"I don't want to go back," I said.

"Why not?"

"My mother and my sister are in Austria," I said. "And I want to join them there." Actually I had no idea where they were but I certainly did not want to go back to communist Russia.

As he rose to leave he said impatiently, "I'm not asking you *if* you want to go. I'm telling you, you *have* to go. Be ready by ten o'clock tomorrow morning."

Deeply disturbed, I told the doctor about the Russian Commissar's visit. "I will not allow it," he said. "The camp where they'll take you is filled with pregnant girls who were raped by Russian soldiers. You're too good for them."

The following morning, the doctor told me to stay in bed; he'd take care of the Russians.

When they came to call on me, he told them, "Annie is too sick to travel today. She has a very high temperature. Better come back another day."

After they'd gone, he told me to dress quickly for he'd come up with a plan of escape for me. "I've contacted a friend who smuggles people across the border into Austria," he said. "You've been a great help to me, and I will do all

I can to help you now." I'm not sure how he managed it, but the doctor supplied me with the necessary papers and money and I was ready to go.

Just as I was leaving sick bay, Herman, a man I had worked with, brought me a letter. "My family doesn't know that I'm still alive," he said. "Would you deliver this letter to my wife, please? She is living with my brother near Graz, Austria. I know they'll take good care of you." Of course! It was comforting to know I had a contact in a foreign country and possibly even a place to live until I could get my bearings.

On the train I met a girl who was also going to Austria to search for her family. We decided to travel together. Miraculously, the border guards allowed us to cross without incident.

We stepped off the train into Austria and freedom!

But there was nobody waiting for us. An icy winter wind chilled us to the bone. We found shelter in a broken boxcar beside the train track. The following day, my friend prepared to walk to a refugee camp in hopes of finding her family. "Come with me," she said. "Maybe you will find your mother and sister there."

But I shook my head no. I had a letter to deliver.

Herman's wife was overjoyed to receive a letter from her husband. His brother, likewise, showed great pleasure. They invited me to eat with them and stay the night. As I snuggled under the warm comforter, I felt so lucky to have found friendly people in a foreign country. I felt certain that they would hire me. I would be sure to tell them that they wouldn't have to pay me; I would work for room and board. But the next morning when I offered my services, Herman's brother said, "We don't need help." His abrupt manner made it clear he wanted me to leave. But where to? "Go to the neighbors," he said. "They may need your help."

Off I trudged over fields covered in snow to a farm house about one kilometer away. It was bitterly cold and my flimsy coat couldn't keep out the wind. Tears blinded my eyes and froze on my eye lashes. How could people be so heartless? Yes, I looked like a tramp with my shabby coat and army boots and I was still limping, but I was willing to work hard. What if nobody hired me? Where would I go? "God, I have nobody but You," I prayed. "Please, help me find favor with some farmer."

At the next farmhouse, a heavy-set woman opened the door a crack. When I told her why I had come, she invited me inside the foyer. "Wait here, while I talk with my husband," she said. On a wall hung a crucifix. As I stared at Jesus on the Cross, tears welled up in my eyes. Yes, Jesus was here too; He would help me.

A small girl about six and her younger brother kept peering at me from behind a door. "Mama, the lady looks so sad," I heard the little girl saying, "please, let her stay."

And so, because of the kindness of a little girl, I was hired. I worked very hard cleaning out pig barns, washing laundry on a scrub board, cleaning the house, taking care of the children and, in the spring, helping the farmer on the field.

But as time went on, I became restless to find my family. I wrote letters to the Red Cross and to a girlfriend who had worked in a hotel in Maurach, Austria, during the war. She might still be there. But no answer came. *She has probably moved on with the rest of the refugees*, I concluded. What else could I try? It began to look hopeless that I would ever find my family again.

One evening, the farmer's wife called out, "Anna, there's somebody at the door for you." Me? Who could be calling? I peered into the darkness trying to identify a man and a woman standing at the door. "Anna, don't you recognize us?" the woman asked.

As I looked more intently into their faces, I recognized them: Suzie Sawatzky and Peter Pauls, from Nieder-Chortitza! They had heard about me through the hotel to which I had written. Now they had come to ask me about their missing relatives. Well, I had no news for them, but they had wonderful news for me: They knew where my mother, my sister, and my nephew were. In a refugee camp in Treffling, not far away.

On a beautiful day in May, 1947, two years after our separation, I was reunited with my family again. What a joyous reunion that was! We had so much to tell each other...

Appendix II:
Mennonite History

THE MENNONITES ARE a Protestant group of believers dating back to the time of the Reformation. They were first called "*Anabaptists*" meaning "again baptized," because of their belief that a person should be baptized upon a personal confession of faith in Jesus Christ. Some converts who had been baptized as infants were being rebaptized, drawing fierce criticism from the Roman Catholic church.

The Anabaptist movement began in Switzerland. Christians discovered the Bible afresh. New converts were examined and then baptized as adults, either by sprinkling or by immersion, and received into the fellowship of the church. Their attempt was to reproduce and practice the apostolic form of church life. They stressed a no-nonsense approach to faith: don't just preach it, live it! And that is still very much their way of serving humanity: with numerous humanitarian projects all over the world.

Since Mennonites refused to hold office or bear arms in warfare, they were severely persecuted almost from the beginning. They were driven from their homes, banished, imprisoned and some were sentenced to death.

The Anabaptist movement spread rapidly from Switzerland to Germany, the Netherlands, Austria, Bohemia and Moravia.

When the Anabaptist movement began to grow in the Netherlands, Menno Simons, a Dutch Roman Catholic priest was converted to their beliefs. In 1536 he renounced the priesthood and joined the Brethren. He soon became the outstanding leader of the Anabaptists, travelling widely to preach and teach the Brethren. He also wrote many books which were published after his death. Soon his followers were called Mennonites. Today there are Mennonite churches located throughout the world.

As a result of severe persecution, many Mennonites fled into other lands. Some went to England; a large group crossed the Atlantic and settled in Pennsylvania, U.S.A.; while others found refuge in East Prussia where they settled along the Vistula River. There they transformed vast stretches of swampland into a prosperous agricultural area. At first they enjoyed toleration, but during the second half of the 18th Century, they once again came into conflict with the government because of their refusal to join the military service. At that time some Mennonites emigrated to America, while others went to Russia.

Russia had acquired new territories through her wars with Turkey. Empress Catherine II was anxious to settle this area with good farmers. She had seen what the Mennonite farmers had accomplished in Prussia and sent Baron von Trappe, a noted Russian officer, as her personal representative to appeal to the Mennonites to come to her country. She made them quite an attractive offer: 65 desjatin (about 180 acres) of free land for each family. She also promised religious freedom and autonomy of their villages and schools, tax exemption, as well as total exemption from all military service.

According to Mennonite tradition, two deputies, Jakob Hoeppner and Johann Bartsch were appointed by the congregation and sent to Russia to inspect the land and draw up the necessary agreements. Empress Catherine II herself received the men and treated them royally. Her officials travelled with them throughout Ukraine and as far south as Odessa and the Crimea (a peninsula at the Black Sea), and showed them the land where the Mennonites might settle. The men brought home a very favourable report. As a result, 228 Mennonite families left their homes in Prussia and immigrated to Russia in 1788. They travelled in a long trek of covered wagons, on foot and with push carts. They settled in Ukraine on the western shore of the Dnieper River between the cities of Ekaterinoslav (Dnepropetrovsk) and Alexandrovsk (Zaporoshye). In a short while another 118 families were added and more villages were built. This first Mennonite settlement in Russia, established in 1789 became known as the Chortitza settlement or the "Old Colony."Later, other Mennonite colonies were established along the Molotschna River, and in other parts of Russia.

For almost 100 years (1789-1880), the Russian government granted a large measure of self-government to the colonies. Each colony was made up of several villages. For instance, the Chortitza colony was made up of nineteen villages. Each village was ruled by a *schulze* (mayor) whose duty it was to preserve order, to enforce the laws, and to preside over the village meetings. He was responsible to an *oberschulze* (superintendent) who governed the entire colony. He, in turn, answered to an administrative board, composed of a director and two assistants who had been appointed by the Russian government.

The three decades before World War I (1914-1918) were the most prosperous years for the Mennonite colonies in Russia. Many prospered in farming, adding field upon field to their estates. By 1819 the nearly treeless steppes had been planted with 30,000 fruit trees, 35,000 other trees, 1,000 grapevines, and about 25,000 mulberry trees to support a silk industry.

The rapid industrialization of Europe toward the middle of the 19th century and the increasing demand for grain laid the foundation for the expansion of grain farming on the Russian steppes. The Mennonites of Chortitza were leaders in agricultural enterprise, in the discovery of the most suitable variety of grain, and in the production of agricultural machinery. Factories were established which produced plows, drills, wagons, mowers, threshing machines, fanning mills, and steam engines. An expanding grain and milling industry developed.

The Mennonite settlements were well organized. Each village elected its school teacher, apportioned its land (although with the rapid influx of immigrants, the land was soon all gone), and took care of its destitute and poor. In each colony were several *zentralschulen* (high schools) taught by well qualified teachers. General hospitals and a mental hospital, a school for deaf and dumb persons, and other institutions sprang up.

In 1870, the Russian government announced that the Mennonites' special privileges in Russia were ending, and that military conscription would become mandatory by 1880. This greatly alarmed the Mennonites. Being pacifists, they believed that any involvement in the military was wrong. Fortunately, they were able to work out a compromise with the government: In place of military service, Mennonite young men would serve the Russian government in forestry. The colonies would accept all responsibility to erect the barracks, feed and clothe the men, and provide them with transportation.

During this period, many Mennonites looked once more for a new country. At that time, approximately 18,000 Mennonites migrated from Russia to America; 10,000 of them settled in the U.S.A. and 8,000 in Canada. With the outbreak of World War I in 1914, Russians became suspicious of the Mennonites. Fearing that Mennonites might be German sympathizers, they made life difficult for the colonies. The collapse of the czar's government in February 1917 and the coming to power of the Bolshevists (communists) brought an end to the freedom for the Mennonites in Russia.

References:

1. Chortitza Mennonite Settlement (Zaporizhia Oblast, Ukraine http://www.gameo.org/encyclopedia/contents/C4652.html

2. Maria Foth, *Beyond the Border: Maria's Miraculous Pilgrimage*, G.R. Welch Publishing Co, Ltd., Burlington, Ontario, copyright 1981, pages 136-140

3. Dr. Walter Quiring and Helen Bartel, *In The Fullness Of Time, 150 Years of Mennonite Sojourn in Russia*, copyright 1974 by Aaron Klassen, Kitchener, Ontario, printed in Canada by Reeve Bean Limited, Waterloo, Ontario, Canada

4. Peter J. Dyck & Elfrieda Dyck, *Up From The Rubble*, copyright 1991 by Herald Press, Scottdale, Pennsylvania, 15683

5. World Book Encyclopedia, Volume 18, copyright 1978, U.S.A. by World Book–Childcraft International. Inc.